ADDICTIONS
Second Edition

Addictions

Second Edition

Maree Teesson, Wayne Hall,
Heather Proudfoot and Louisa Degenhardt

Psychology Press
Taylor & Francis Group
HOVE AND NEW YORK

First published 2002 by Psychology Press Ltd
27 Church Road, Hove, East Sussex, BN3 2FA, UK

Second edition published 2012 by Psychology Press Ltd
27 Church Road, Hove, East Sussex, BN3 2FA, UK

Simultaneously published in the USA and Canada
by Psychology Press
711 Third Avenue, New York NY 10017

Psychology Press is an imprint of the Taylor & Francis Group, an Informa business

British Library Cataloguing in Publication Data
A catalogue record for this book is available from the British Library

Library of Congress Cataloging-in-Publication Data
Addictions / Maree Teesson . . . [et al.]. – 2nd ed.
      p. cm.
   Prev. ed. entered under Teesson, Maree.
   Includes bibliographical references and index.
   ISBN 978-0-415-58299-5 (hardback)
   1. Substance abuse–Treatment. 2. Substance abuse–Psychological
aspects. 3. Addicts. I. Teesson, Maree. II. Teesson, Maree. Addictions.
   RC564.T44 2011
   362.29–dc23
                                                      2011019525

ISBN: 978-0-415-58299-5 (hbk)
ISBN: 978-0-415-58300-8 (pbk)
ISBN: 978-0-203-11933-4 (ebk)

Typeset in Palatino by Garfield Morgan, Swansea, West Glamorgan
Cover design by Jim Wilkie
Printed and bound in the UK by TJ International Ltd, Padstow, Cornwall

Contents

Series preface

Clinical Psychology: A Modular Course was designed to overcome the problems faced by the traditional textbook in conveying what psychological disorders are really like. All the books in the series, written by leading scholars and practitioners in the field, can be read as stand-alone texts, but they will also integrate with the other modules to form a comprehensive resource in clinical psychology. Students of psychology, medicine, nursing, and social work, as well as busy practitioners in many professions, often need an accessible but thorough introduction to how people experience anxiety, depression, addiction, or other disorders, how common they are, and who is most likely to suffer from them, as well as up-to-date research evidence on the causes and available treatments. The series will appeal to those who want to go deeper into the subject than the traditional textbook will allow, and base their examination answers, research, projects, assignments, or practical decisions on a clearer and more rounded appreciation of the clinical and research evidence.

Chris R. Brewin

Other titles in this series:

Depression, Second Edition
Constance Hammen and Edward Watkins

Stress and Trauma
Patricia A. Resick

Childhood Disorders, Second Edition
Philip C. Kendall and Jonathan S. Comer

Schizophrenia
Max Birchwood and Chris Jackson

Anxiety, Second Edition
S. Rachman

Eating and Weight Disorders
Carlos M. Grilo

Personality Disorders
Paul M. G. Emmelkamp and Jan Henk Kamphuis

Acknowledgements

We would like to acknowledge Dr Vaughan Rees for assistance with the cognitive behavioural intervention for cannabis dependence, Kate Hetherington for research assistance and editing, Andrew Baillie for discussion and thoughtful comments, and the staff of the National Drug and Alcohol Research Centre, University of New South Wales, Sydney, whose research is the cornerstone of this book.

The nature of addiction 1

In developed countries many people will drink alcohol at some time in their lives and a minority will use illicit drugs. Not all who use alcohol and drugs will develop problems with their use but some will and the extent of the problems they experience will differ from person to person. Consider the following scenario:

> Robin is a young male, who goes out on Friday and Saturday nights with his friends. He usually drinks a lot on these occasions, although he doesn't usually drink much during the rest of the week. On a regular night out Robin drinks around 20 drinks over a period of 8 hours until he is fully drunk. Robin's friends, while also drinking, do not drink as much as Robin. Robin's friends are concerned for Robin as he has been involved in a number of pub fights while drunk. He was recently involved in a brawl that resulted in his breaking a stranger's nose and being arrested by the police.

As this example suggests, it is not just drinking alcohol that causes problems but the behavioural consequences of heavy alcohol use. A person is considered to have a problem with alcohol or other drugs when he or she has difficulty controlling their use (Robin drinks until he is fully intoxicated); when obtaining, using, and recovering from alcohol or drugs consumes a disproportionate amount of the individual's time; and when the individual continues to drink alcohol or take drugs in the face of problems that he or she knows to be caused by such use (e.g., brawling in the pub). People typically become tolerant to the effects of alcohol or drugs, requiring larger doses to achieve the desired psychological effect, and abrupt cessation of use often produces a withdrawal syndrome. Many experience other psychological and physical health problems from heavy use. Their alcohol or drug use may adversely affect the lives of their spouses, children, and other family members, friends and workmates.

In summary, problems with alcohol and drug use are characterized by:

- a strong desire to take alcohol or drugs;
- difficulty in controlling use; and
- health, behavioural and social problems attributed to drug and alcohol use.

The key feature is a desire to take psychoactive drugs, alcohol, or tobacco. The desire is often strong and sometimes overpowering. For example:

> Amanda has used cannabis at the weekend for 3 years. Last month she began using it daily. Amanda is 20 years old. She wishes she could resist using cannabis daily but she finds the desire to use the drug overpowering. Her cannabis use is starting to interfere with her life; she is spending a lot of money on cannabis, is arriving late for her job, and is having trouble remembering things.

Why do some people develop problems with alcohol and drugs while others do not? How should we respond to problem alcohol and drug use? These questions are complex and intriguing, so simple answers should not be expected. Addiction is determined by multiple interacting factors, the unravelling of which provides a challenge to addiction research.

What is a drug?

A drug can be defined as a chemical agent, other than food, that affects biological functioning in humans or other animals. A psychotropic drug is one that acts in the brain to alter mood, thought processes, or behaviour. Table 1.1 presents a list of commonly used psychotropic drugs and some of their "street" names. There are very many street names for drugs that can vary from country to country.

TABLE 1.1

A brief list of "street" drug names (USA, UK, and Australia)

Drug type	Common names
Cannabinoids	Afghan, bhang, bud, columbian, doobie, cones, dope, chronic, ganja, gold, grass, hash, head, hemp, herb, hooch, hydro, jay, jive, joint, kif, marijuana, mary jane, mexican, MJ, mull, pot, reefer, shit, skunk, smoke, spliff, THC, weed
Cocaine	Base, blow, C, Charlie, coca, coke, crack, dust, dynamite, flake, gold dust, heaven dust, lady, nose, nose candy, Peruvian, rock, snow, speedball (heroin and cocaine), toot, white dust, zip
Amphetamines	Bennies, blue angels, cat, crank, crystal, dexies, ice, jollies, meth, pep pills, shabu, speed, uppers, whizz
Ecstasy	E, eccy, XTC, pills, eggs, doves, MDMA
Opioids: Analgesics and others	Brown, black (opium), codeine, DOA, doloxene, H, hard stuff, heroin, horse, junk, methadone, morphine, mortal combat, percodan, pethidine, poppy, scat, skag, smack, tar
Hallucinogens and psychedelics	Acid, blotters, blue dots, blue meanies, goldtops, ketamine, LSD, magic mushrooms, mesc, microdot, psilocybin, special K, tabs, trips, white lightening
Inhalants and solvents	Amyl, bulbs, ethyl, glue, laughing gas, petrol, nitrous oxide, poppers, rush, snappers
Sedatives and tranquillizers	Amies, blue birds, blue devils, blue heaven, blues, bullets, candy, dolls, barbiturates, barbs, downers, downs, librium, mogadon, normison, quads, rohypnol, serepax, sleepers, sleeping pills, trangs, yellows, valium, xanax
Phencyclidine (PCP)	Angel, green tea, K, mist, purple rain, super, whack

For example, the website for the US Office of National Drug Control Policy (ONDCP) provides a comprehensive list of street names used in the US (ONDCP, 2010).

The current *Diagnostic and Statistical Manual of Mental Disorders* (DSM-IV) has defined a number of classes of drugs that may be part of a substance use disorder (American Psychiatric Association [APA], 1994). These are, in alphabetical order: alcohol, caffeine, cannabis, hallucinogens, heroin and other opiates, inhalants, nicotine, phencyclidine (PCP), sedatives and stimulants (cocaine and amphetamines). Since the publication of DSM-IV, the use of the stimulant drug ecstasy has increased considerably and so it will also be discussed in this book.

Effects of drugs

Each class of drugs has different short-term or immediate effects and longer-term effects. These effects can differ from person to person, depending on a person's size, their frequency of drug use, the potency of the drug being consumed, their health status and many other factors. The short-term and long-term effects are outlined below for each of the major classes of drugs.

- *Alcohol:* The short-term effects of alcohol include loss of inhibitions, lack of coordination and slower reaction time, blurred vision and slurred speech, aggression. Excessive use of alcohol can result in coma and death from respiratory or heart failure.
- *Nicotine:* The short-term effects of nicotine include increased pulse rate, temporary rise in blood pressure, acid in the stomach, decreased blood flow to body extremities (such as fingers and toes), nausea, and watery eyes. The long-term use of nicotine can reduce a person's sense of smell and taste, produce premature and abundant face wrinkles, and increase the risk of colds, chronic bronchitis, emphysema, heart disease, and certain types of cancer.
- *Cannabis:* The short-term effects of cannabis include euphoria, increased talking and laughing, sleepiness, loss of coordination and concentration, loss of inhibitions and a feeling of well-being. It can also cause bloodshot eyes, anxiety and paranoia, increased appetite and dryness of the mouth and throat. The long-term use of cannabis can lead to dependence, increased risks of respiratory diseases associated with smoking, decreased learning and memory abilities, decreased motivation in areas such as study and work, decreased concentration and accidental injury.
- *Heroin:* The short-term effects of heroin include euphoria, relief of pain, and a feeling of well-being. Heroin use can also result in nausea and vomiting, constipation, and sleepiness. The long-term effects include lowered sex drive, impotence in men and infertility in women, risk of hepatitis and AIDS through injection, death by overdose. The effects of heroin are described in this quote:

> After you fix it you feel the rush, like an orgasm if it's good dope. Then you float for about four hours; nothing positive, just a normal feeling, nowhere. It's like being half

asleep, like watching a movie; nothing gets through to you, you're safe and warm. The big thing is you don't hurt. You can walk around with rotting teeth and a busted appendix and not feel it. You don't need sex, you don't need food, you don't need people, you don't care. It's like death without permanence, life without pain.

(Case study of Ed from Smith & Gay, 1972, p. 145)

- *Cocaine:* The short-term effects of a stimulant such as cocaine include increased blood pressure, heart rate, breathing rate and body temperature, increased alertness and energy, an extreme feeling of well-being, sexual arousal, dilated pupils, and loss of appetite. The long-term effects of cocaine include sleeping disorders, sexual problems, heart attacks, strokes and respiratory failure, as well as nosebleeds, sinusitis and tearing of the nasal wall resulting from snorting, and hepatitis or human immunodeficiency virus (HIV) through sharing injecting equipment.
- *Amphetamines:* The short-term effects of amphetamines include euphoria and a feeling of well-being, restlessness, sleeplessness, irritability and aggressiveness, increased blood pressure and pulse rate, sweating, a dry mouth, nausea and anxiety. The long-term effects of amphetamines include sleeping problems, appetite suppression, high blood pressure, and rapid and irregular heart beat. Frequent heavy use can lead to symptoms of psychosis such as paranoia, delusions, hallucinations and bizarre behaviour ("amphetamine psychosis", Druginfo Clearinghouse: The drug prevention network, 2010)
- *Ecstasy:* The short-term effects of ecstasy include euphoria or feelings of well-being, increased self-confidence, lack of inhibition, sweating and nausea, increased blood pressure and heart rate, increased anxiety and insomnia, teeth grinding, tongue and cheek chewing and dry mouth. Less research has been carried out on the long-term effects of heavy ecstasy use but there is suggestive evidence that some long-term users experience depression and also memory and cognitive impairment (Degenhardt, Bruno, & Topp, 2010a).

People use different drugs for many reasons although most report that the main reason they do so is to "feel better". Not everyone who uses drugs, including alcohol, will be adversely affected, so why do some people who use drugs develop problems while others do not? This is the focus of the next section.

What are the causes of problems with alcohol and other drugs?

There is a continuing debate among researchers about what causes addiction and problems related to the use of alcohol or other drugs: Is it a "chronic disease" or a behaviour learnt from your family or peers? Addiction has come to be viewed by many persons who have recovered from addiction as a chronic disease. An individual was considered to have the disease if he or she lacked the willpower to stop the excessive use of alcohol and other drugs. The only cure, according to many who hold this view, is complete abstinence from alcohol or other drug use.

By contrast, modern learning theories see addiction as the consequence of chronic heavy alcohol or drug use. This heavy use is argued to arise from an interaction between an individual's genes and his or her environment. Once the person develops a pattern of heavy drug use, the risk of addiction increases.

The first step in unravelling addiction is to define clearly what is meant by the term "addiction". What does it mean to say that a person has a problem with alcohol or drugs? In 1970, Griffith Edwards and colleagues provided a clinical description of alcohol dependence (Edwards, Arif, & Hodgson, 1981; Edwards & Gross, 1976; Edwards, Gross, Keller, Moser, & Room, 1977). They suggested that "alcoholics" exhibited a characteristic cluster of symptoms the presence of which could be used to diagnose addiction to alcohol. They developed this concept after carefully observing the problem drinkers they had seen in their treatment clinics. The symptoms they observed included a strong desire to drink, needing to drink more alcohol to get the same effect, and experiencing withdrawal symptoms when the intake of alcohol stopped.

A related concept of dependence on many drugs was then included in the *Diagnostic and Statistical Manual of Mental Disorders*. According to the DSM definition, dependence was defined as a compulsion to use a drug that was not medically necessary, and the use of which was accompanied by impaired health or social functioning (APA, 1994; World Health Organization, 1993). The term "drug dependence" as used in these classifications was intended to be equivalent to the more popular term "addiction".

Edwards et al. (1977) suggested that alcohol dependence could be defined by a repeating cluster of signs and symptoms that occurred in heavy drinkers and could be conceptually distinguished from alcohol-related problems. Seven factors were regarded as major symptoms of alcohol dependence:

1 Narrowing of the behavioural repertoire: For example, an individual who is dependent may only drink one or two types of alcoholic drink in the same way and the same quantities on weekdays and weekends.
2 Salience of drinking or drug use: With increasing dependence the individual gives greater priority to using the substance than to other activities.
3 Subjective awareness of a compulsion: The individual experiences a loss of control over the substance use, and finds themselves unable to stop using the substance.
4 Increased tolerance: The individual needs to use more of the substance to get the same effects.
5 Repeated withdrawal symptoms: These may include: fatigue or exhaustion, sweating, diarrhoea, anxiety, depression, irritability, restlessness, trouble sleeping, tremors, stomach ache, headache, weakness, nausea or vomiting, fits, muscle aches or cramps, runny eyes or nose, yawning, intense craving, seeing things that are not really there, heart beating fast, change in appetite, fever.
6 Relief or avoidance of withdrawal symptoms by further drinking: The individual uses alcohol in order to relieve withdrawal symptoms (e.g., morning drinking).
7 Reinstatement of dependent drinking after abstinence: There is a rapid return to dependent drinking after a period of abstinence.

Since Edwards et al., other research on the description and classification of problems with alcohol has found that the dependence concept fits well with clinical reality. Furthermore, and importantly, a similar concept has been shown to apply to many other drugs of dependence (APA, 1994). These classification systems are outlined below and form the basis of internationally agreed criteria for diagnosing problems associated with alcohol and other drugs.

Diagnosing problems

One of the most widely used classificatory system for psychological disorders is the DSM-IV (APA, 1994). This provides the criteria for diagnosing drug abuse and drug dependence that are outlined below. It is currently being revised and version 5 is due for release in 2013. It is proposed that the section on substance-related disorders will be changed such that these disorders will be rated along a single continuum with graded severity (Proudfoot, Baillie, & Teesson, 2006; Teesson, Lynskey, Manor, & Baillie, 2002). For example, alcohol dependence and abuse will be subsumed under "alcohol use disorder", using a scoring system based on most of the current criteria. It is proposed to remove the legal criterion (the third criterion in Abuse, see below) and to incorporate a criterion assessing craving; this applies to all other drugs in the current DSM-IV (APA, 2010). The issue of what thresholds will be considered to indicate level of disorder (moderate or severe) is currently being researched (e.g., Mewton, Slade, McBride, Grove, & Teesson, 2011).

Diagnosing abuse

Criteria for substance abuse

A. A maladaptive pattern of substance use leading to clinically significant impairment or distress, as manifested by one (or more) of the following, occurring within a 12-month period:

(1) recurrent substance use resulting in a failure to fulfil major role obligations at work, school, or home (e.g., repeated absences or poor work performance related to substance use; substance-related absences, suspensions, or expulsions from school; neglect of children or household)

(2) recurrent substance use in situations in which it is physically hazardous (e.g., driving an automobile or operating a machine when impaired by substance use)

(3) recurrent substance-related legal problems (e.g., arrests for substance-related disorderly conduct)

(4) continued substance use despite having persistent or recurrent social or interpersonal problems caused or exacerbated by the effects of substance (e.g., arguments with spouse about consequences of intoxication, physical fights).

B. The symptoms have never met the criteria for substance dependence for this class of substance.
(American Psychiatric Association, 1994, pp. 182–183)

Diagnosing dependence

To qualify for a diagnosis of drug dependence in the DSM-IV system, at least three of seven key symptoms must be met in the past year. The key symptoms for diagnosis of drug dependence are outlined below. In addition to outlining the criteria that relate to substance dependence generally, DSM-IV also describes the specific aspects of dependence for 11 classes of substances.

Criteria for substance dependence

A maladaptive pattern of substance abuse, leading to clinically significant impairment or distress, as manifested by three or more of the following, occurring at any time in the same 12-month period:

(1) tolerance, as defined by either of the following:
   (a) a need for markedly increased amounts of the substance to achieve intoxication or desired effect
   (b) markedly diminished effect with continued use of the same amount of the substance
(2) withdrawal, as manifested by either of the following:
   (a) the characteristic withdrawal syndrome for the substance
   (b) the same (or a closely related) substance is taken to relieve or avoid withdrawal symptoms
(3) the substance is often taken in larger amounts or over a longer period than was intended
(4) there is a persistent desire or unsuccessful efforts to cut down or to control substance use
(5) a great deal of time is spent in activities necessary to obtain the substance, use the substance (e.g., chain smoking), or recover from its effects
(6) important social, occupational, or recreational activities are given up or reduced because of substance abuse

(7)   the substance use is continued despite knowledge of having a persistent or recurrent physical
or psychological problem that is likely to have
been caused or exacerbated by the substance.
(American Psychiatric Association, 1994, p. 176)

The experience of dependence and abuse on a drug can be very different for different individuals and across different drug classes as is illustrated in the following cases:

Ecstasy abuse: Dana is a university student who takes ecstasy most weekends when she goes out clubbing with friends. Despite trying to limit the amount she spends on drugs, she often spends money meant for food and bills on pills for a night out. When this happens Dana ends up borrowing money for food until she next gets paid. Dana often skips classes on Mondays to recover from her weekends of clubbing.

Alcohol dependence: Jeff is a 26-year-old male who presented to his general practitioner (GP) because he had been missing work to recover from hangovers. He is married with two children. His wife encouraged him to ask his GP about his drinking. Jeff had begun drinking at the age of 15 years and became a regular drinker at 18 years. By the time he was 20, he was drinking four to six beers a day during the week and more on Friday and Saturday nights. In the last year he had begun binge drinking on weekends; that is, drinking up to 15 or more standard drinks. He has also been drinking the next morning in order to recover.
  His current alcohol use during the week is two standard drinks of beer before work, eight at lunch and another five after work. His GP did a medical examination and analysed his liver enzymes. While Jeff's liver was not enlarged, a number of liver enzymes were elevated.

Problem drug use can be sporadic, as in the case of Dana, or more chronic and long term, as with Jeff's drinking. Both are experiencing problems that are affecting not only themselves but also their friends, work, and family. Many people will use alcohol and drugs, some will experience problems, and others will not. A person may be having a problem with drugs if he or she has:

- a strong desire to take alcohol or drugs;
- difficulty controlling use; and/or
- associated problems due to drug and alcohol use.

The amount of use that is acceptable to different cultural groups and cultures varies, as does acceptance of associated problems. This is particularly the case for alcohol. While there are no norms for safe levels of use for illicit substances, many countries have developed guidelines for the safe consumption of alcohol. The cultural and societal aspects of alcohol use are considered in the next section, but first we present a quick quiz that is useful in assessing problems with cannabis in young people entitled the Cannabis Problems Questionnaire for Adolescents, Short Form (CPQ-A-S, reproduced with permission from Elsevier; Proudfoot, Vogl, Swift, Martin, & Copeland, 2010, p. 736).

Are you on the road to cannabis addiction?
Answer the following questions as honestly as you can:
1. Have you tended to smoke more on your own than you used to?
2. Have you worried about meeting people you don't know when you are stoned?
3. Have you spent more time with smoking friends than other kinds of friends?
4. Have your friends criticised you for smoking too much?
5. Have you found yourself worried about the amount of money you have been spending on cannabis?
6. Have you been in trouble with the police due to your smoking?
7. Have you been physically sick after smoking?
8. Have you passed out after a smoking session?
9. Have you had pains in your chest or lungs after a smoking session?
10. Have you had a persistent chest infection or cough?
11. Have you felt paranoid or antisocial after a smoking session?
12. Have you worried about getting out of touch with friends or family?

An answer of "Yes" to 3 or more of the above questions indicates marijuana use may be problematic.

Cultural factors and attitudes to drugs

The drinking and drug-taking behaviour of individuals and societies always occurs in the context of social norms, attitudes, and values and there are variations between cultural groups in the types of substances and the level of their use that is socially acceptable (Heath, 2000). Attitudes to alcohol provide a good example of these variations. In some societies – for example, in Moslem countries such as Saudi Arabia, Bangladesh and Iran – it is illegal to drink alcohol. In other societies – for example, in France – it is expected that everyone will drink, and individuals who do not do so are considered unusual. Within Anglo-Celtic cultures, significant proportions of drinkers, especially young drinkers, drink to get drunk on a regular basis. These behaviours are much less commonly found in Mediterranean countries, despite the fact that alcohol consumption is high in these countries.

Cultural variations in what is an acceptable level of alcohol intake are reflected in the guidelines for moderate drinking that are published by governments in countries around the world. To cite the extremes, the Australian National Health and Medical Research Council recommends daily consumption of no more than 20 g of ethanol equivalents per day for both men and women in order to reduce lifetime risks of harm, while in the Basque Country of Spain, the Department of Health and Social security defines daily consumption of 70 g of ethanol equivalents for both men and women as acceptable (International Center for Alcohol Policies, 2010).

This book focuses on the following five major classes of drugs: alcohol, nicotine, cannabis, opioids, and stimulants. Problems with the use of these drugs have the greatest social and economic impact on society, and their use also contributes to many life-threatening disorders. The term 'drug' is used hereafter to encompass all five groups of substances. Other illegal drugs and non-drug addictions, such as problem gambling, eating, and sexual behaviour, are not addressed in this book.

Who becomes addicted? 2

For many years, addiction was considered to be a relatively rare disorder with a poor outcome: few individuals were thought to become abstinent, and many died from the medical complications of their drug use. As these views were mostly formed from studies of people who sought treatment, they were biased towards more severe disorders among the minority of addicted individuals who seek treatment for addiction. More recently, a number of large epidemiological studies of addiction in the general population have challenged these pessimistic views in suggesting that addictive disorders are much more common disorders, the majority of which remit. The results of some of these studies are reported below.

The US Epidemiologic Catchment Area study

The Epidemiologic Catchment Area (ECA) study was the first large epidemiological study to examine problems with alcohol and other drugs in the general community. It involved personal interviews with 20,000 Americans in Baltimore, Maryland; Los Angeles, California; New Haven, Connecticut; Durham, North Carolina; and St Louis, Missouri (Regier et al., 1990; Regier, Narrow, Rae, Manderscheid, Locke, & Goodwin, 1993; Robins & Regier, 1991). A standardized interview for detecting the presence or absence of mental disorders was used for 40 major psychiatric diagnoses that included alcohol and drug dependence.

In this study, a diagnosis of *alcohol abuse* required excessive or uncontrolled alcohol use and impairment in social or occupational functioning due to alcohol use. *Alcohol dependence* required evidence of either excessive or uncontrolled drinking, or social and occupational impairment (or both), and evidence of either tolerance or withdrawal (or both), consistent with the DSM-IV criteria (APA, 1994) described in Chapter 1. Alcohol use disorders (alcohol abuse and/or dependence) were the second most common mental disorder in the survey (Helzer, Burnam, & McEvoy, 1991).

One in seven people had had an alcohol use disorder at some time in their lives. As expected, men were more likely than women to have an alcohol use disorder (24% of men and 5% of women) at some time in their lives. Alcohol use disorders were more common in younger people (Helzer et al., 1991) and the more an individual drank (exposure to heavy drinking) the greater their risk of developing an alcohol use disorder. The lifetime experience of a disorder increased from 15% among all drinkers to 49% of those with a history of drinking more than seven drinks in a session at least once a week. Differences in exposure to heavy drinking probably explain the differences in lifetime rates between men and women and younger and older persons. Men were much more likely to experience heavy drinking and, with changes in social values, younger people were also more likely than older people to have been exposed to heavy drinking.

Other mental disorders, such as depression and anxiety, were also common in people with alcohol use disorders, nearly half of whom (47%) also had a second psychiatric diagnosis. The most common such diagnoses were: drug abuse and dependence, antisocial personality disorder, mania, schizophrenia, panic disorders, and obsessive–compulsive disorders (Helzer et al., 1991).

Alcohol dependence in the ECA was "a disorder of youthful onset", with 80% of those who ever developed a disorder experiencing their first symptom before the age of 30. It was also a disorder with a high rate of remission: half of those who had ever had a disorder had not experienced any symptoms for at least a year. The average duration of symptoms was less than 5 years, indicating that many who drink heavily and experience symptoms of dependence can stop drinking for periods of a year or more. Importantly, most individuals who stopped or moderated their drinking did so without professional assistance. Only 12% had ever told a doctor about their drinking problem.

This large epidemiological study showed that alcohol use disorders in the community have a more benign outcome than the pessimistic picture we obtain from clinical populations, which contain a preponderance of individuals who have been unable to stop drinking on their own.

The ECA study also estimated the prevalence of drug abuse and dependence in the community. Illicit drug use was defined as "any non-prescription psychoactive agents other than tobacco, alcohol and caffeine, or inappropriate use of prescription drugs" (Anthony & Helzer, 1991, p. 116). Individuals had to have used an illicit drug on more than five occasions before they were asked about symptoms of drug abuse and dependence.

A diagnosis of *drug abuse* required a pattern of pathological use and impaired functioning (defined in the same way as alcohol abuse). A diagnosis of *drug dependence* required only tolerance or withdrawal (except in the case of cannabis, where a diagnosis of dependence required pathological use, or impaired social functioning, and either tolerance or withdrawal). The problem had to have been present for at least 1 month.

One in three in the ECA sample (36%) had used one or more illicit drugs at some time in their life. Cannabis was the most commonly used illicit drug (having been used by almost one in three Americans). Drug abuse and dependence (hereafter drug use disorders) were diagnosed in 6% of the population, with cannabis affecting 4% of the population, followed by stimulants (2%), sedatives (1%), and opioid drugs (0.7%). Men had higher rates of drug use disorders than women, and the highest rate was in the 18 to 29-year age group.

As was true of alcohol use disorders, exposure to illicit drug use was the most likely reason for the differences in rates between men and women and younger and older persons. The low rates of drug use disorders among adults over the age of 40, in part, reflected recent widespread illicit drug use in US society.

There was also a high rate of other mental health problems among those with drug use disorders. Over two-thirds (76% of men and 65% of women) had a second psychiatric diagnosis. The most common diagnoses were alcohol use disorders (60% of men and 30% of women) and antisocial personality disorder (22% of men and 10% of women).

Little information was provided on the remission of drug use disorders because of the relative youth of this group, and hence the shorter duration of their disorders. As with alcohol use disorders, only a minority of those who had a diagnosis of drug use disorders had mentioned their drug problem to a health professional.

Later community surveys from developed countries

Since the ECA, several large-scale nationally representative mental health surveys have been carried out in developed countries. It is difficult to compare prevalence findings between many of these surveys because different versions of the DSM and different sampling and methodologies have been used. However, as the following discussion reveals, similar trends exist cross-nationally with regard to who becomes addicted to drugs and alcohol.

The USA

In the USA, the National Comorbidity Survey (NCS, Kessler et al., 1994), the NCS Replication (Kessler, Chiu, Demler, Merikangas, & Walters, 2005), and the National Epidemiological Survey on Alcohol and Related Conditions ((NESARC, Grant et al., 2004b) are large-scale surveys that have produced a wealth of information on drug and alcohol disorders. In general these surveys have supported the findings of the ECA study.

The major findings with regard to drug and alcohol disorders in the USA from the most recent US survey (NESARC) are listed below.

- Having an alcohol abuse or dependence disorder in the past 12 months is associated with being male, white (cf. blacks, Asians and Hispanics), young and unmarried and being in the lowest socioeconomic group (Hasin, Stinson, Ogburn, & Grant, 2007).
- Lifetime and past 12 months alcohol dependence was strongly and significantly associated with the presence of comorbid psychiatric and other drug disorders, i.e., any mood, anxiety or personality disorder, nicotine dependence and any other drug use disorder. This association remained significant once socio-demographic variables and other comorbidities were controlled.
- Only 12% of those with alcohol dependence in the past 12 months received alcohol treatment in that period. A majority did not receive any treatment or attend self-help groups (Cohen, Feinn, Arias, & Kranzler, 2007). People with comorbid mood, person-ality, and other drug use disorders were more likely to seek treatment.
- For people with drug dependence, sociodemographic associa-tions were similar to those with alcohol dependence. Further,

comorbidity of the full range of other psychiatric disorders remained significant after controlling for sociodemographic and other psychiatric disorders. Although higher than for alcohol dependence, treatment for drug dependence, at 31%, was also disappointingly low (Compton, Thomas, Stinson, & Grant, 2007). Again, psychiatric comorbidity was associated with treatment seeking.

- Nicotine dependence was independently associated with all other psychiatric disorders measured in NESARC (Grant, Hasin, Chou, Stinson, & Dawson, 2004a). Persistent nicotine dependence was associated with having severely disruptive life events in the past 12 months. It is unclear whether stressful life events have a causal effect on smoking or whether common risk factors predispose an individual to both smoke and be exposed to more stressful situations (Balk, Lynskey, & Agrawal, 2009). Similarly, NESARC also indicated that nicotine dependence accounts for some of the increased risks of psychopathology associated with problem gambling.

The UK and Europe

The most recent population-based mental health survey carried out in England, Scotland and Wales found that people with alcohol and drug disorders were also more likely to be young and male. It also found relatively low levels of health service use among these groups (Singleton, Bumpstead, O'Brien, Lee, & Meltzer, 2001). Similar results were found in the Netherlands Mental Health Survey and Incidence Study (NEMESIS, Bijl, Ravelli, & van Zessen, 1998), as well as the European Study of the Epidemiology of Mental Disorders (ESEMeD, Alonso et al., 2004). The latter surveys also found high levels of comorbid mental disorders that predicted health service use.

The New Zealand Mental Health Survey

In 2003–2004 New Zealand conducted a mental health survey with a particular interest in examining ethnic differences in the prevalence of disorders and service use. Almost 13,000 adults aged 16 and up were interviewed for this survey (Wells, Oakley Browne, Scott, McGee, Baxter, & Kokaua, 2006). Substance use disorders in New Zealand were more common among males, young people and socio-economically disadvantaged people. Comorbidity with other mental disorders overall was high, and comparable with other developed countries (Scott, McGee, Browne, & Wells, 2006). After adjusting for age and socioeconomic background, the prevalence of substance use disorders was approximately double among the Maori compared with the rest of the population. Service usage for all those with substance use disorders was low overall and lower still in the Maori ethnic group (Wells et al., 2006).

The Australian National Surveys of Mental Health and Well-Being

In 1997, the first Australian National Survey of Mental Health and Well-Being (NSMHWB, Hall, Teesson, Lynskey, & Degenhardt, 1999b) examined the prevalence of common mental disorders in the Australian adult general population. The survey interviewed a representative sample of 10,641 adults (aged 18 years or older) from throughout Australia and assessed symptoms of the affective, anxiety, and substance use disorders. Substance use disorders included abuse and dependence on alcohol and tobacco, and abuse and dependence on four classes of drug: cannabis, stimulants, sedatives, and opioids.

The survey found that substance use disorders were more common among males than females, reflecting the higher rates of exposure of adult males to heavy alcohol and drug use (Andrews, Hall, Teesson, & Henderson, 1999). The prevalence of drug and alcohol disorders steadily declined with age for both males and females. Approximately 1 in 6 Australians aged 18–24 had a substance use disorder compared with only 1 in 90 for those 65 and over. This decline can be attributed largely to high rates of remission of these disorders, with some contribution from substance-related mortality. Other interesting age-adjusted correlates were:

- substance use disorders were more likely to occur among those who were living alone than those who were married or in a *de facto* relationship;
- the prevalence of substance use disorders was higher among people who were unemployed than those who were employed or not in the labour force (i.e., not seeking work);
- people born in Australia and other English speaking countries had higher levels of substance use disorders than those born in non-English speaking countries;
- the prevalence of substance use disorders was not associated with level of education or with urban/rural status in Australia.

As in other surveys, this Australian study found low levels of service use for those diagnosed with substance use disorders: about 1 in 7 sought help for their disorder in the previous 12 months. Levels of comorbidity were high: just under a half of females with a substance use disorder also had a comorbid anxiety or affective disorder; while about a quarter of males did. Those with comorbid mental disorders had significantly higher use of health services.

Tobacco dependence was also associated with having an affective or anxiety disorder (Degenhardt, Hall, & Lynskey, 2001). Almost a third of current smokers had a mental disorder, which is twice the rate of those who never smoked. Current smokers were four times more likely to have another substance use disorder, three times more likely to have an affective disorder and twice as likely to have an anxiety disorder compared with lifelong non-smokers. This does not mean that smoking causes these disorders – having a mental illness is also a risk factor for smoking (Australian Bureau of Statistics, 2008).

In 2007 a second Australian NSMHWB was conducted (NSMHWB2, Slade, Johnston, Oakley Browne, Andrews, & Whiteford, 2009). The methodology used in this second survey differed from the first survey, which means that prevalence levels cannot be directly compared. However, this latter survey used a similar methodology to more recent surveys from comparable countries such as New Zealand, the USA and European countries. In terms of correlates of substance use disorders, this second survey confirmed findings from the first Australian survey as well as those from comparable countries (Teesson et al., 2010).

Summary

The epidemiological surveys tell us much about who becomes addicted. Across different countries the surveys consistently show that men are much more likely than women to have a substance use disorder, probably because they are exposed to heavier alcohol use and more drug taking. The studies also show that, contrary to popular belief, alcohol dependence is experienced by the young at greater rates than older persons because it is a disorder of youthful onset (younger than 30 years). Disorders among young adults have high remission rates.

The high levels of comorbidity among people with substance use disorders, combined with the greater likelihood that comorbid individuals seek treatment, underlines the need for drug and alcohol treatment agencies to assess and treat comorbid disorders – particularly the more common mood and anxiety disorders. Guidelines for treating comorbid psychiatric disorders in alcohol and other drug services are available on the National Drug and Alcohol Centre website at http://ndarc.med.unsw.edu.au/comorbidity.

The health consequences of alcohol and other drug use and dependence 3

Introduction

Drug users who become dependent on alcohol and other drugs are at high risk of experiencing adverse consequences of their drug use, including health problems directly due to drug use, violence, and accidents. However, the relationship between dependence and harm to health is not perfect. Not all drug-dependent persons develop serious adverse health consequences and adverse consequences of use are not confined to dependent users. For example, healthy young adults may drink heavily enough to meet criteria for alcohol dependence but cease their hazardous use of alcohol before health complications develop and accidental injuries, drowning, falls, and violence may occur among intoxicated people who are not alcohol or drug dependent.

The following overview summarizes the major adverse health consequences that have been linked to the use of alcohol and other drugs using data from the 2000 Global Burden of Disease by Rehm, Taylor, and Room (2006). This study estimated the harm caused by alcohol, tobacco, and illicit drug use using a combined measure of mortality and disability, namely, the disability-adjusted life year (DALY). DALYs combine the years of life lost due to premature death with years of life lost due to disability attributable to a specific risk factor such as alcohol or drug use. Measurement of the effects of a substance on mortality and morbidity is based on epidemiological and other evidence that there is a causal relationship between the risk of exposure and death and disability. The strength of the causal relationship is estimated from meta-analyses of epidemiological data.

Exposure is measured differently for the different substances. With alcohol, it is based on average volume and frequency of self-reported alcohol consumption obtained from survey and key informant studies. For illicit drugs and tobacco, it is based on survey data on frequency of use, with the understanding that there is considerable uncertainty with these data. For tobacco, estimates of exposure are mostly based on birth and death registration data combined with the assumption that excess deaths due to lung cancer are attributable to tobacco smoking, which applies in most parts of the world (Rehm et al., 2006).

Global Burden of Disease (GBD) data also present findings for three world socioeconomic regions:

1   developed countries, e.g., USA, Europe, Japan, Australia;
2   developing countries, with low population mortality, e.g., China, South-East Asia, much of South America and the Middle-East; and
3   developing countries, with high mortality, e.g., much of Africa, India, Pakistan.

In terms of the burden of disease attributable to substance use, tobacco caused more deaths worldwide than alcohol and illegal drugs combined, and this was true within regions as well. The more developed the region, the higher the death rate from tobacco and the same was true for illicit drugs. The picture was a little more complicated for alcohol because it has purported beneficial effects on mortality at low-consumption levels that are more pronounced in developed countries with high rates of cardiovascular disease. Deaths attributed to alcohol were higher in the developing countries that have low mortality such as the emerging economies in Asia and South America (Rehm et al., 2006). The smaller contribution of drugs and alcohol to mortality and morbidity in less-developed countries reflects the larger contribution to death and disability of poor nutrition and sanitation than in developed countries. Tobacco and alcohol contribute almost equivalent amounts to the global disease burden (approximately 4% of the total GBD). This is because DALYs take into account the fact that alcohol causes more disability and death at a younger age than tobacco. Illicit drugs contribute approximately one-fifth of that of alcohol or tobacco (0.8%).

In general, the more developed the region, the higher the DALYs attributed to these substances. The increased impact of alcohol on GBD can be explained by the higher rates of death and disability that occur at a younger age in alcohol users. Death and disability related to tobacco occur later in life and thus contribute less to the DALYs tally. Rehm et al. (2006) also demonstrate that for each of the substance groups, males are four or more times likely to be affected than women.

Alcohol-related mortality and morbidity

An earlier review by Rehm and colleagues (Rehm, Gmel, Sempos, & Trevisan, 2003) (see Table 3.1 below) summarized the impact of alcohol on chronic health conditions.

The review classified males and females into light, moderate, and heavy drinkers and indicated the relative risks of developing various diseases for each category of alcohol use. Alcohol use disorders were not listed because they are 100% attributable to alcohol use. Although known to be associated with alcohol use, major depression was not included because the appropriate research has not been done to estimate relative risk. The relative risk is the risk compared with abstainers. For example, female moderate drinkers have an 85% higher risk of developing mouth and oropharynx cancers than female abstainers. In fact, the risk of all malignant neoplasms is increased for all three levels of drinkers and in a dose–response manner. It is equivalent for both males and females (except for breast cancer in males, which was indeterminate). Similarly the risk is increased for cirrhosis of the liver, with moderate to heavy drinkers having almost 10 times greater risk than abstainers. Risk for epilepsy among drinkers is also higher than among abstainers, with male and female moderate and heavy drinkers around seven times more likely to have the condition. Risks for male and female drinker categories tended to be equivalent in all the above-mentioned conditions.

The picture is less clear-cut with diabetes and cardiovascular diseases (CVD). For most categories of CVD, the relationship between alcohol use and CVD was a J-shape, with abstainers being more likely to develop CVD than light to moderate drinkers. On current data, drinking 20 g of alcohol a day provides the best protection against

TABLE 3.1

Relative risk for major chronic disease from alcohol use (adapted from Rehm et al., 2003)

Daily alcohol consumption	Females			Males		
	Light (0–19.99 g)	Moderate (20–39.99 g)	Heavy (40 g+)	Light (0–39.99 g)	Moderate (40–59.99 g)	Heavy (60 g+)
Malignant neoplasms						
Mouth and oropharynx cancers	1.45	1.85	5.39	1.45	1.85	5.39
Oesophagus cancer	1.80	2.38	4.36	1.80	2.38	4.36
Liver cancer	1.45	3.03	3.60	1.45	3.03	3.60
Breast cancer	1.14	1.41	1.59			
• Under 45 years of age	1.15	1.41	1.46			
• 45 years and over	1.14	1.38	1.62			
Other neoplasms	1.10	1.30	1.70	1.10	1.30	1.70
Diabetes mellitus	0.92	0.87	1.13	1.00	0.57	0.73
Neuropsychiatric conditions						
Epilepsy	1.34	7.22	7.52	1.23	7.52	6.83
Cardiovascular diseases						
Hypertensive disease	1.40	2.00	1.40	1.40	2.00	4.10
Coronary heart disease	0.82	0.83	1.12	0.82	0.83	1.00
Cerebrovascular disease						
Ischaemic stroke	0.52	0.65	7.98	1.27	2.19	2.38
Haemorrhagic stroke	0.59	0.65	7.98	1.27	2.19	2.38
Other CVD causes	1.50	2.20	2.20	1.50	2.20	2.20
Digestive diseases						
Cirrhosis of the liver	1.26	9.54[a]	9.54[a]	1.26	9.54[a]	9.54[a]

[a] For liver cirrhosis, moderate and heavy drinking categories were combined.

coronary heart disease; it is not until 70 g a day that drinking becomes riskier than abstaining. However as Rehm et al. (2003) point out, this protective effect at low to moderate levels tends to be based on *average* drinking, and so does not take into account patterns of drinking. It is likely that the protective effect of alcohol use may apply to populations where drinking is regular rather than episodic. Recent research suggests that binge drinking may be more harmful than regular drinking in its effects on coronary heart disease, heart attacks, and stroke. However, more research evidence is required on this issue. Drinking alcohol with food has been found in some studies to reduce risks of coronary heart disease. Research on the type of alcoholic beverage (e.g., wine versus beer) has not shown differential effects on chronic disease risk (Rehm et al., 2003).

Maternal alcohol use can result in fetal alcohol syndrome (FAS), which can significantly impact the child's health and development. FAS is a leading cause of intellectual disabilities and has been estimated to occur in 0.5 to 2.0 cases per 1000 live births in the United States (May & Gossage, 2001).

Alcohol use is also associated with acute risks to health, most often from accidental injuries and interpersonal violence. In developed countries, alcohol-related traffic accidents are a major contributor to the burden of disease due to alcohol. For example in the USA, Hingson and Winter (2003) found that alcohol was a factor in 41% of deaths in traffic accidents in 2002, and that deaths from traffic accidents (drivers, passengers, or pedestrians) were more likely in young and middle-aged adults. The male:female relative risk was 1.62 (46% cf. 29%). Other research in the USA has found that alcohol is involved in around 40% of other unintended deaths, such as burns, drowning, falls, and poisoning (Gmel & Rehm, 2003).

Alcohol is also involved at significant levels in crimes involving aggression by and towards others, including fights and brawls in public places, as well as spousal and child abuse and sexual assault. This link between alcohol use and interpersonal violence has been found to be not so much causal, as an association. Longitudinal studies have found that level of aggression has been found to be a persistent characteristic from childhood to young adulthood and this suggests that early aggressive behaviour predicts both alcohol abuse and the aggressive behaviour later in young adulthood (Gmel & Rehm, 2003). Australian researchers have also concluded, in relation to domestic violence, that it is not the alcohol as such that causes the behaviour – a non-aggressive person does not become aggressive under the influence of alcohol (Nicholas, 2005). Instead personality, environmental factors, and social cues mediate the relationship between alcohol and violence.

The level of alcohol use by victims of family violence is also positively related to the amount of persistent trauma from such violence (Kaysen, Dillworth, Simpson, Waldrop, Larimer, & Resick, 2007). In summary, although there is a clear association between alcohol use and aggressive behaviour, a causal relationship has not been clearly established in people who are not normally aggressive.

Tobacco-related mortality and morbidity

According to the World Health Report (World Health Organization [WHO], 2002), tobacco caused almost 5 million premature deaths in the year 2000 – over 1 million more than in 1990. The increases in use and harms occurred mainly in developing countries, especially among young people, where tobacco use is described as an epidemic. It is estimated that if current trends continue, by 2020, approximately 10 million people will die annually as a result of tobacco smoking. This includes 7 million people from developing countries. Overall, smokers have death rates two to three times higher than non-smokers of the same age.

The number of cancers caused by tobacco use include lung cancer, cancer of the oral cavity, pharynx, oesophagus, stomach, liver, pancreas, larynx, nose, bladder, kidney, cervix, as well as myeloid leukaemia (Davis, Wakefield, Amos, & Gupta, 2007). Smokeless tobacco use increases the risk of cancers of the oral cavity and pancreas. The GBD estimated that 12% of both ischaemic heart disease and stroke were attributable to smoking. Approximately 80–90% of the 2.2 million deaths worldwide in 1990 from chronic obstructive pulmonary disease (COPD) were attributable to smoking, with the number of deaths due to COPD expected to reach 4.7 million in 2020. Studies have found approximately 30–40% of morbidity and mortality from tuberculosis is attributable to smoking. Smoking in pregnant women also contributes to preterm birth, small size for gestational age, reduced birth weight and stillbirths. This also applies to smokeless tobacco use (Davis et al., 2007).

Passive smoking also has significant implications for health. It has been found to cause lung cancer, nasal sinus cancer, breast cancer, heart disease mortality and morbidity, acute lower respiratory tract infections in children, asthma, middle ear infections, low birth weight, sudden infant death syndrome, and preterm delivery (Davis et al., 2007).

Illicit drug-related mortality and morbidity

The major contribution that illicit drug use makes to burden of disease is via premature death. Illicit drug users are approximately 13 times more likely to die prematurely than their peers (Hulse, English, Milne, & Holman, 1999). There are four main causes for this elevated death rate: drug overdose, HIV/AIDS, suicide, and trauma (Degenhardt, Hall, Warner-Smith, & Lynskey, 2004). In addition to causing premature death, these outcomes also contribute to disability and increased demand on health services. HIV/AIDS occurs as a consequence of sharing contaminated injecting equipment. Similarly, unclean practices in injecting drug use can lead to hepatitis B and C infection, which also increases morbidity and mortality.

We do not know as much about the causal relationships between illicit drug use and health as we do about tobacco and alcohol. Direct, acute drug effects such as drug overdose and drug-induced psychosis are known but their contribution is probably under-estimated because of underdiagnosis. The contribution of illicit drugs to chronic disease and injury is probably also underestimated because of the paucity of data on the long-term effects of their use (Hall & Degenhardt, 2009).

Illicit drug use accounts for a smaller number of deaths than alcohol and tobacco but produces a larger number of life years lost per death because many of these deaths occur among illicit drug users in their 20s and 30s. Hospitalization attributable to illicit drug use is also concentrated in the same young age groups, with the addition of the adverse effects of maternal drug use on the health of babies and infants (Hall & Degenhardt, 2009).

The most recent analysis of the burden of disease and injury in Australia found that illicit drug use accounted for 2% of the total burden (Begg, Vos, Barker, Stevenson, Stanley, & Lopez, 2007). Almost three-quarters was experienced by males, with the major causes contributing to this burden via mortality and morbidity including HIV/AIDS, hepatitis, low birth weight, inflammatory heart disease, poisoning, suicide, and other self-inflicted injuries. These factors also contribute to increased demand on health services. As illicit drug users age, the longer-term effects of their use will be reflected in the effects of chronic hepatitis B and C infection (Begg et al., 2007).

Adverse health and psychological effects of cannabis use

Although cannabis overdose has not been found to cause deaths in humans, there are a number of acute and chronic effects of cannabis use that impact the health of users. The major acute psychological and health effects of cannabis intoxication are: anxiety, dysphoria, and panic in naïve users (Hall, Degenhardt, & Lynskey, 2001); and cognitive and psychomotor impairment while intoxicated, leading to an increased risk of accidental injury if an intoxicated person drives a motor vehicle or operates machinery (Hall & Degenhardt, 2009; McLaren & Mattick, 2007).

Chronic cannabis use is likely to produce dependence as manifest in a loss of control over cannabis use (Hall & Degenhardt, 2009). Chronic cannabis use is also likely to lead to an increased risk of chronic bronchitis, impaired respiratory function, and possibly respiratory cancers. Evidence is also suggestive that chronic heavy use leads to cardiovascular disease and psychotic symptoms, especially where there is a personal or family history of such disorders. Some studies have found negative effects of heavy cannabis use on educational attainment in adolescents, as well as an increased likelihood of using other drugs; but the explanation of these associations is contested.

Studies in animals have found that exposure to Δ-tetrahydrocannabinol (THC) can cause reduced fertility, birth defects, and low birth weight. However, because of the influence of significant confounders, such as co-occurring alcohol and tobacco use, these findings have not been clearly supported in studies on humans. Where such confounders have been controlled, outcomes indicate that using cannabis in pregnancy is likely to reduce birth weight (McLaren & Mattick, 2007).

Adverse health and psychological effects of psychostimulant use

Amphetamines and cocaine

Cocaine and amphetamines can cause death through seizures, cardiac arrythmias and respiratory failure. These can occur irrespective of route of administration, dose of drug or frequency of drug use. Most deaths are accounted for by cardiovascular complications. Even a small amount of cocaine can be fatal in naïve users. Short-term cardiovascular events include chest pain, palpitations, tachycardia and hypertension. In the longer term the use of psychostimulants predicts premature and accelerated development of coronary artery atherosclerosis, which in turn can increase the risks of coronary thrombosis and stroke. When methamphetamine and cocaine are used together, the cardiotoxic effects are greater than either drug used alone. Mixing psychostimulants with other drugs, such as heroin or alcohol, also increases the risks to physical health (Darke, Kaye, McKetin, & Duflou, 2007). Where psychostimulants are injected there are increased risks of contracting blood-borne infections such as HIV and hepatitis. Psychostimulant use is also associated with increased risky sexual behaviours and their sequelae (Queensland Health, 2004).

Dependence on psychostimulants is common among regular users, with reports of up to 50% of regular users of amphetamines and cocaine being dependent. Dependence on these psychostimulants is more likely with more frequent use, higher doses of drug and smoking or injecting the drug (Darke et al., 2007).

Ecstasy

According to a large-scale review by Rogers and colleagues (2009), ecstasy use on its own is rarely fatal. Over three-quarters of deaths in ecstasy users were in polydrug users. Where deaths and hospitalizations occurred solely from ecstasy use, they appeared to be due to hyperthermia or hyponatraemia (ingestion of large amounts of fluid affecting the sodium balance in extracellular fluid). Other reported fatalities and hospitalizations were due to cardiovascular and neurological dysfunction and suicide. Other acute effects of ecstasy use include acute psychiatric effects, urinary retention and respiratory problems.

Among the longer-term harms of ecstasy are deficits in neurocognitive function – in particular in verbal and working memory (Rogers et al., 2009). Self-rated depression, memory, and impulsivity are also higher among ecstasy users, but it is unclear whether this association is causal because these studies are methodologically compromised. Dependence on ecstasy has not been established, but a minority of users express concern about their use and seek medical help (Degenhardt et al., 2010a).

Adverse health and psychological effects of heroin use

The adverse health consequences of heroin use include: heroin dependence; blood-borne infectious diseases through sharing injecting equipment; and premature mortality from overdose, violence, and accidents (Teesson, Mills, Ross, Darke, Williamson, & Havard, 2008).

The major causes of harm from the use of heroin are fatal and non-fatal overdose. In Australia the rate of fatal overdoses rose from 36.6 per million population in 1988 to a peak of 101.9 per million in 1999. This rate had declined steadily and appears to have remained stable from 2003 at around 32 per million (Degenhardt, Roxburgh, Black, & Dunn, 2006). Non-fatal heroin overdose is common among regular heroin users, with between 45 and 65% of such users reporting a non-fatal overdose at some time in their 10-year histories of use (Darke & Ross, 1997; Stafford et al., 2006).

The typical fatal overdose victim in Australia and most other developed countries is a single, unemployed male of approximately 30 years, who is a long-term dependent heroin user who was not in treatment at the time of death. There is a strong association between a fatal and a non-fatal overdose and the concomitant use of alcohol and benzodiazepines. Contrary to popular conception, fluctuations in heroin purity do not wholly explain the number of overdose fatalities. Variations in the user's opiate tolerance appear to be more important (Ross, 2007).

Blood-borne viruses, primarily HIV and hepatitis B and C are spread by the injection of heroin and other drugs. Studies of injecting drug users in Australia have found that the prevalence of hepatitis C infection was 50%, with higher rates among injectors over the age of 25 years, and in persons who have injected for more than two years or been imprisoned in the previous year. The rate of new hepatitis C infections is estimated at around 15% per year in Australian injecting drug users. Between 30 and 60% of Australian injecting drug users have antibodies to hepatitis B. As with hepatitis C, older users have a higher prevalence, with rates over 80% among those seeking treatment. Despite known risks of needle sharing, 11% of injecting drug users in Australia in 2005 reported that they had used a needle after someone else, and 17% said they had passed on a used needle to someone else (Stafford et al., 2006).

Studies have repeatedly shown that heroin-dependent individuals have high rates of psychological disorders, with the most common being depression, anxiety disorders, and antisocial personality disorder (Ross, 2007). Heroin users are also over-represented among the homeless (Teesson, Hodder, & Buhrich, 2003).

Controversies on the positive effects of alcohol and cannabis

Over recent decades there has been considerable controversy about the possible health benefits of alcohol and the therapeutic use of cannabis. Many population studies have shown a J-shaped association between the use of alcohol and mortality. In other words, people who drink moderately (one or two drinks per day) have a reduced risk of death compared with those who do not drink at all. The risk of death, however, increases if a person drinks heavily. Studies have demonstrated that much of the reduction in mortality arises from reduced coronary artery disease with moderate alcohol consumption.

The area is controversial because the alcohol industry has been quick to publicize the positive effects of alcohol use. Thun et al. (1997) examined both the adverse and beneficial effects of alcohol consumption in 490,000 men and women over 30 years of age, between 1982 and 1991. A slightly reduced overall mortality with moderate alcohol consumption (up to one or two drinks of alcohol daily) was reported, confirming the findings of previous studies. More specifically, rates of death from all cardiovascular diseases combined were 30–40% lower among men and women reporting at least one drink daily than that found in non-drinkers. However, it is not known how long moderate alcohol consumption must continue for this benefit to occur.

A large-scale longitudinal study from Sweden was reported by Theobald and colleagues (Theobald, Johansson, Bygren, & Engfeldt, 2001) that used a random sample from the population and objective outcome measures obtained from hospital and death records. They compared low- and high-risk drinkers with moderate drinkers (not abstainers). There was some controversy about comparing drinker categories with abstainers as the 'abstainer' may have been a drinker in the past and gave up for health reasons, or may have other health-based reasons for abstaining. Despite this difference in methodology, the study by Theobold et al. (2001) had similar findings to previous studies – heavier drinkers and light drinks had poorer health outcomes than moderate drinkers. They also found that, in general, the alcohol-related diseases causing death were the same as those causing disability (in this case, hospitalization). This suggests that alcohol may be a causative factor in these diseases.

Despite some generally positive effects being demonstrated for chronic illness by low to moderate alcohol consumption, it appears that even moderate alcohol use increases the risk of some cancers, particularly breast cancer in women (Allen et al., 2009). Furthermore, studies of the impact of alcohol use on motor vehicle accidents suggest that any alcohol consumption before driving significantly increases the risk of death and injury from accidents (Heng, Hargarten, Layde, Craven, & Zhu, 2006). A recent review by Chikritzhs, Fillmore, and Stockwell (2009) has also argued that much of the positive findings for moderate alcohol use on coronary heart disease could be due to sample selection and misclassification of abstainers and occasional drinkers. Their review found that many study participants are excluded from research based on ill health that significantly limits generalization to the broader population. Further, alcohol usage can vary throughout the lifetime, recall of alcohol usage is suspect, and effects of patterns of drinking have not been examined sufficiently. A recent study by Roerecke and Rehm (2010) demonstrated that moderate drinking interspersed with occasional binge drinking (five drinks per occasion) removed any positive cardiovascular effects of moderate drinking. It is therefore important that the apparent protective effects of alcohol be treated with due scepticism pending better quality research in the area.

The therapeutic use of cannabis has also been the focus of considerable debate (Royal College of Physicians, 2005). There are a number of medical conditions for which cannabis may be of medical benefit:

- HIV-related wasting and cancer-related wasting;
- pain unrelieved by conventional treatment;
- neurological disorders including multiple sclerosis, Tourette's syndrome, and motor neurone disease;
- nausea and vomiting that, in cancer patients undergoing chemotherapy, does not respond to conventional treatments.

There are two major challenges in using cannabis for therapeutic purposes. First, cannabis is a crude plant product that contains a complex mixture of many chemicals. This makes production of a standard cannabis-based medicine difficult. Cannabis smoke also contains a variety of substances that are dangerous to health. Second, the legal issues present major challenges. Those who are opposed to the medical use of cannabis are concerned about the social implications, particularly the possibility that medical use may promote recreational use. However, research from the USA suggests that introducing medical cannabis does not increase its overall use as a recreational drug (Gorman & Charles Huber, 2007). A number of countries have adopted a compassionate regime so that those suffering from the range of illnesses listed above can use cannabis without facing criminal sanctions.

Summary

Persons who become dependent on alcohol and other drugs are at higher risk of experiencing adverse health and other consequences. Among the greatest acute risks are accidental injury, drowning, car accidents, falls, violence, and death by overdose in the case of heroin. Drug and alcohol use place the individual at significant risk for chronic diseases such as cardiovascular disease, blood-borne viruses, and several cancers. Not all drug-dependent persons develop serious health consequences. There is also some evidence that cannabis may have some medical uses and that moderate use of alcohol can have positive health benefits in middle-aged adults at high risk of cardio-vascular disease.

Theories of addiction: Causes and maintenance of addiction

4

Overview: Theories of addiction

In attempting to explain why people become dependent on drugs, theories tend to emphasize either psychobiological or psychosocial approaches. Psychobiological approaches include both neurobiological and genetic explanations of addictive behaviour. Psychosocial approaches focus on explanations that involve learning models and individual differences, usually while taking into account the cultural and environmental factors that make drug dependence more likely. There are a variety of theories regarding the question of why people become dependent on drugs, and it is likely that these are not mutually exclusive. It is clear that we need an approach that synthesizes these perspectives to have the greatest explanatory value (West, 2006).

Physiological bases of addiction

Neuroscientific theories

Neuroscience with the aid of neuroimaging is gradually revealing how the brain changes as a consequence of the regular use of drugs. These changes suggest that chronic drug use produces persistent impairments in neurocognitive and motivational states (Carter, Capps, & Hall, 2009).

Neuroscientific theories require an understanding of the effects of drugs on the brain. Box 4.1 outlines the actions of each of the major drug classes. Different drugs have different primary actions on the brain, but two major pathways – the dopamine reward system and the endogenous opioid system – have been implicated as being common to the effects of most drugs of dependence (Koob & Le Moal, 2008; Nutt, Robbins, Stimson, Ince, & Jackson, 2007).

Dopamine reward system

Neuroimaging has identified the multiple brain systems that are affected by psychoactive drug use. It is hypothesized that changes in these systems may explain the behaviour of drug-addicted people, specifically, their loss of control and compulsive drug taking, and their difficulty in sustaining abstinence and avoiding relapse to drug use. The dopaminergic pathway has dense connections to the forebrain and the higher cognitive centres of the frontal cortex. Although it is not the only neural system in the brain affected by drug abuse, changes in these pathways are considered to be central to the development and maintenance of addictive behaviour (Carter et al., 2009).

Administration of drugs of abuse directly or indirectly increases dopamine levels in the nucleus accumbens located in the medial forebrain. Dopamine release is believed to motivate repetition of the behaviour that precedes it. Some addictive drugs produce more than 10 times the dopamine released in the nucleus accumbens by natural reinforcers, making drug use much more rewarding than daily activities such as eating and sex (Carter et al., 2009). Although this dopamine surge was originally thought to be the neurobiological correlate of reward or pleasure produced by drug use, it is now considered as a signal of the "salience" of an event.

"Salience" may not only signal a rewarding stimulus; it may also apply to aversive, novel, and unexpected stimuli (Goodman, 2008). This may explain why drugs such as the psychostimulants are associated with pleasure or euphoria while nicotine is not; and why drugs that originally produced euphoria continue to be used when their effects are no longer rewarding (Goodman, 2008).

Dopamine response decreases with chronic drug use as neural pathways adapt to the effects of the drug. The brain adaptively responds to overstimulation by decreasing the number of neurones that are able to respond to dopamine. This reduces the overall responsiveness of the dopamine reward system and deprives everyday activities of their salience. After drug taking ceases, the decreased

BOX 1.1 Molecular and cellular sites of drug action

Alcohol

Alcohol (ethanol) has inhibitory and excitatory effects on the brain. Its inhibitory effects are mediated by its action on γ-aminobutyricacid (GABA)-A receptors, whilst its excitatory effects are mediated by glutamate receptors, especially N-methyl-D-asparate (NMDA) receptors (World Health Organization, 2004b). Both glutamate and GABA-A probably mediate the sedating effects of alcohol as well as memory impairment while intoxicated. GABA-A receptors in distinct brain regions have been found to be involved in the acute effects of alcohol as well as in the development of tolerance and dependence. They also mediate the effects of poor motor coordination and lowered anxiety. The reinforcing effects of alcohol are likely due to a combination of increased dopamine activity in various parts of the brain produced by activation of the GABA system and stimulation of endogenous opioid release (World Health Organization, 2004b).

Nicotine

Nicotine activates the acetylcholine nicotinic receptor producing increased release of the neurotransmitters acetylcholine, noradrenaline (norepinephrine), dopamine, serotonin, glutamate, beta-endorphin and GABA (Benowitz, 2008; Markou, 2008).

Cannabis

The psychoactive effects of cannabis primarily come from the ingredient Δ^9-tetrahydrocannabinol (Δ^9-THC), that activates two cannabinoid receptors: CB-1, largely located in the central nervous system, and CB-2, which is located in the peripheral tissues in the immune system and in the brain (World Health Organization, 2004b). Δ^9-THC produces its effects by acting on CB-1 receptors to prevent uptake of acetylcholine, noradrenaline, dopamine, 5-hydroxy-tryptamine, GABA, glutamate, and aspartate. CB-2 receptors have a lesser role in addiction, and mainly regulate immune responses.

Opiates

The brain's endogenous opioids, endorphins and enkephalins, are released to mediate endogenous opiate actions (Altman et al., 1996; Nutt, 1997). Opiate drugs stimulate at three major opiate receptor subtypes: mu, delta, and kappa. The mu receptor appears to be the subtype most involved in the reinforcing effects of opiate drugs (World Health Organization, 2004b). Mu receptors are located on cell bodies of dopamine neurones in the ventral tegmental area, the origin of the mesolimbic dopamine system; and on neurones in the basal forebrain, particularly the nucleus accumbens (Altman et al., 1996; Di Chiara & North, 1992). The delta agonists also produce rewarding effects but less than mu agonists (World Health Organization, 2004b). They may potentiate the effects of reinforcers on behaviour (Altman et al., 1996). The kappa opiate receptors and the endogenous enkephalins appear to be involved in the aversive effects of the opiate withdrawal syndrome (Altman et al., 1996; World Health Organization, 2004b).

Psychomotor Stimulants

Cocaine

Cocaine binds to dopamine, noradrenaline, and serotonin transporters (Altman et al., 1996). It appears to produce its reinforcing and psychomotor stimulant effects by blocking dopamine reuptake at the synapse. Dopamine D1-like receptors play an important role in the euphoric and stimulating effects of cocaine. Support for this comes from research demonstrating that D1 antagonists attenuate the euphoric and stimulating effects of cocaine, and reduce the desire to take cocaine in cocaine-dependent persons (Romach et al., 1999; World Health Organization, 2004b).

Amphetamine

Amphetamine directly stimulates the release of dopamine independently of neuronal excitation (unlike cocaine that blocks its reuptake). Amphetamines probably also inhibit the reuptake of the catecholamines and directly stimulate catecholamine receptors, increasing overall activity (World Health Organization, 2004b).

Ecstasy

Ecstasy or MDMA (3,4-methylenedioxymethamphetamine) is thought to act upon serotonin, dopamine, and noradrenaline. It primarily blocks the reuptake of serotonin but also increases the release of dopamine (World Health Organization, 2004b).

responsiveness of the dopamine system explains the sense of loss, depression, and withdrawal that often follows abstinence. The physical changes to the reward system may also explain why people can resume their addictive drug use months or years after becoming abstinent (Carter et al., 2009).

The research in this area is very much in its infancy and the nature and level of contribution of dopaminergic systems to addictive behaviours requires considerable further research. The role of other neurotransmitters that have been associated with drug-taking behaviour – the endogenous opioids, glutamate, and γ-aminobutyric acid (GABA) – also need to be better understood, including their interactions with dopamine (Goodman, 2008).

Endogenous opioid system

The brain's endogenous opioid system also plays an important role in drug use and misuse. Exogenous opiates such as heroin, morphine, and codeine all act as opiate receptor agonists; tolerance rapidly develops to their effects with repeated use. Adaptation of opiate receptors occurs quite readily after chronic opiate use, as is demonstrated by the need for larger amounts to achieve pain relief or euphoria. Administration of the opiate antagonist, naloxone, quickly induces withdrawal symptoms in chronic opioid users.

The opioid system is also involved in the rewarding effects of other psychoactive substances, including alcohol. The opiate antagonist naltrexone, for example, reduces the reinforcing properties of alcohol (see Chapter 5). Regular tobacco smoking may also produce changes in the responsivity of the endogenous opioid system thereby increasing the likelihood of developing nicotine dependence (Drews & Zimmer, 2010; Krishnan-Sarin, Rosen, & O'Malley, 1999). Naloxone can also attenuate the rewarding effects of Δ^9-THC (Gardner, 1992). Goodman (2008) has recently summarized evidence that all drugs of abuse, and naturally rewarding behaviour such as eating and sexual activity, are followed by the release of endogenous opioids.

The dopaminergic and opioid systems have been hypothesized to play different roles in addictive behaviour. The dopaminergic pathway is said to be associated with the incentive, preparatory aspects of reward, which are experienced as thrill, urgency, or craving (salience). The opioid system, by contrast, is associated more with the hedonic aspects of reward, such as the feelings of enjoyment that follow use of a drug (Le Merrer, Becker, Befort, & Kieffer, 2009).

Neuroadaptation

There is evidence that changes in synaptic plasticity are involved in the development and maintenance of addiction. Such changes may underpin craving, impaired impulse control and relapse to drug use (Carter et al., 2009). These neuroadaptations occur in the mesolimbic dopaminergic pathway and in other limbic regions, such as the prefrontal cortex. Chronic drug administration has thus been implicated in neural changes that affect executive control, cognitive ability, memory, learning, habits, and homeostatic mechanisms. All of these impair decision making about drug use, facilitating continued drug use and relapse after abstinence (Carter et al., 2009).

Koob and Le Moal (1997, 2008) have proposed a theory of drug dependence based on neuroadaptation: a theory of neural opponent motivation. According to this theory, neuroadaptation occurs in response to the acute effects of repeated drug administration. It may be of two types: *within-system adaptations*, in which the changes occur at the site of the drug's action, and *between-system adaptations*, in which changes in different mechanisms are triggered by the drug's action. Repeated drug administration produces changes in the chemistry of the brain that oppose the drug's effects. When drug use is discontinued, these adaptations are no longer opposed and the brain's homeostasis is disrupted (Carter et al., 2009). On this hypothesis, tolerance to the effects of a drug, and withdrawal when drug use stops, are both the results of neuroadaptation. Animal models have also shown that stressful stimuli activate the dopamine reward system, explaining why relapse so often occurs in response to stress as an attempt to avoid withdrawal-like symptoms (Koob & Le Moal, 2008).

Traditionally, conceptualizations of drug dependence have focused on the motivating effects of physical withdrawal symptoms. More recent formulations concentrate on the presence of motivational symptoms, such as dysphoria, depression, irritability, and anxiety. These hypothesize that negative motivational symptoms are manifestations of neurobiological changes that signal "not only . . . the beginning of the development of dependence, but may also contribute to vulnerability to relapse and may also have motivational significance" (Koob & Le Moal, 1997, p. 53). This approach hypothesizes that chronic drug use produces changes in the dopamine reward system and the endogenous opioid system.

Recent evidence on brain development also offers insights into how addiction develops. The developing brain is restructured during adolescence with significant remodelling of both grey and white matter continuing until the mid-20s (Lubman, Yucel, & Hall, 2007). Late developing parts of the brain include the superior temporal gyrus (concerned with memory, object recognition, and audio-visual inputs) and the dorsolateral prefrontal cortex (concerned with impulse control, judgement, and decision making) (Lenroot & Giedd, 2006).

The neurocognitive evidence suggests that heavy drinking may affect the normal development of these areas in the brain in ways that are correlated with poorer verbal and non-verbal working memory. These deficits persist into adulthood, with alcohol use in adolescence correlated with poor visuospatial performance 8 years later (Tapert, Caldwell, & Burke, 2005). More large scale studies of this sort are needed (preferably on epidemiologically derived samples) to improve our understanding of the effects that the most widely used drugs, alcohol, nicotine, and cannabis, have on the developing adolescent brain (Hall, Degenhardt, & Teesson, 2009).

Genetic factors

Genetic theories attempt to explain which individuals develop drug dependence. They assume that people differ in their genetic likelihood (*vulnerability*) of using and developing dependence on drugs. Individual differences in vulnerability to develop drug dependence have been examined, in family, adoption, and twin studies (e.g., Bierut et al., 1998; Kendler, Davis, & Kessler, 1997; Merikangas et al., 1998), and more recently in studies of specific "candidate" genes that may underlie vulnerability to dependence.

Twin and adoption studies indicate that vulnerability to drug addiction runs in families, and that environmental and genetic factors also play a role. Depending on the substance, it has been estimated that the variance in risk of developing dependence that can be attributed to genetic factors is 40–70% (Carter et al., 2009).

Genetic factors may influence vulnerability to addictive behaviour in a variety of ways. This may be: via individual differences in sensitivity to drug effects (e.g., metabolic factors); personality characteristics that increase the likelihood of using drugs (e.g., impulsivity, novelty seeking); and individual differences in how rewarding the effects of drugs are to the individual. Thus, an individual who is genetically disposed to have a more intense and rewarding drug experience may be more likely to become dependent once they have tried a drug; if they do not have easy access to the drug, however, then their risk of addiction may be low. If drugs are available, then an individual who has less impulse control may be more likely to initiate drug use, but may be less likely to proceed to dependence if they do not find the drug's effects rewarding (Skinner & Aubin, 2010).

Specificity of drug effects

Do individuals have a vulnerability towards developing dependence on specific drugs, or is there a general vulnerability to develop dependence on any psychoactive substance? Merikangas and colleagues (1998) found that substance use disorders were more common among relatives of people with substance use disorders compared with relatives of a control group. Other research involving male twins has also examined the issue of a common genetic vulnerability to substance misuse (Kendler, Jacobson, Prescott, & Neale, 2003; Kendler, Myers, & Prescott, 2007; True et al., 1999; Tsuang et al., 1998).

Two recent reports by Kendler and colleagues (2003, 2007) used samples of twins, to study the specificity of these effects. Their initial study looked only at male twins and only at illicit substance use. They concluded that neither shared genetic nor shared environmental experiences could explain which *type* of drug was favoured – differences in types of drug used in vulnerable individuals were best accounted for by the unique experience of the individual in their particular environment. Their second study used both male and female twins and included illicit drugs (cannabis and cocaine) as well as alcohol, nicotine, and caffeine. They identified two genetic factors, one loading on the illicit drugs, and the other on licit drugs. The relatively high correlation between these factors suggested that they had some degree of genetic vulnerability in common as well as specific genetic vulnerabilities. The authors suggested that the genetic factors that distinguished dependence liability on licit and illicit drugs were associated with personality and impulsivity, which related to an individual's willingness to experiment with illegal drugs.

Identifying specific risk genes

Attempts to identify specific genes that may explain addictive liability has not so far been particularly successful. In their review, Carter and colleagues (2009) concluded that it is likely that many genes make small individual contributions to the genetic risk of addiction. Particular genetic profiles also interact with different environmental influences (stress, peer pressure, etc.) producing highly varied outcomes in individual addictive behaviour.

Psychosocial theories

Psychological explanations of drug dependence have often been based on concepts that explain other compulsive or impulsive behaviours, such as obsessive-compulsive disorder or gambling (Miller, 1980). In particular, emphasis has been given to impaired control over drug use or behaviour, and continuation of drug use despite problems arising from it. A variety of psychological approaches to drug dependence include learning and conditioning (behavioural models), cognitive theories, pre-existing behavioural tendencies (personality theories), and models of rational choice.

Behavioural theories

Behavioural theories of addiction are based on two learning paradigms – operant and classical conditioning, both of which may occur outside conscious control. Operant conditioning (instrumental learning) explains addictive behaviour as being under the control of its consequences (reinforcers) (West, 1989). Drug self-administration is an example of *instrumental behaviour* because the activities of persons (or animals in an experiment) are instrumental in obtaining the consequences (the drug's effects). People can become addicted through positive reinforcement (e.g., where the pleasurable effects of a drug act as a reward); or through negative reinforcement (e.g., in order to avoid the aversive effects of drug withdrawal) (West, 2006).

Other behavioural theories of addiction focus on the role of Pavlovian or *classical conditioning* in the development and maintenance of addictive behaviours. *Cue exposure theory*, for example, argues that cues are important in the development and maintenance of addictive behaviour (Drummond, Tiffany, Glautier, & Remington, 1995; Heather & Greeley, 1990). A cue that has previously been present when drugs were administered will come to elicit conditioned responses (cue reactivity) that are thought to underlie craving. This may explain why someone who was dependent on a substance continues to experience strong cravings after they have been abstinent for some time.

The cues that may be associated with addictive behaviours can vary. Exteroceptive cues occur before the use of a drug, and may include the smell of an alcoholic drink, the sight of a needle, or even the time of day when drugs are typically taken. Interoceptive cues include such things as the effects of a drug on the brain's receptors, depressed affect (Greeley, Swift, & Heather, 1992), or beliefs about drug effects (Drummond et al., 1995).

The response to these cues may be autonomic, behavioural, or symbolic–expressive (Drummond et al., 1995). Autonomic responses in cue exposure experiments include changes in heart rate, skin temperature, and salivation; symbolic expressive responses include self-reported drug-craving and urges to use drugs; and behavioural responses include an increased likelihood of using drugs.

Social learning theory incorporates the operant conditioning paradigm while taking into account individual motives, inherited traits, prior learning, and current life circumstances. For example, a person who takes up drugs because of peer pressure faces different issues when trying to overcome addiction than someone who takes drugs to solve a social problem (West, 2006). The relapse prevention model of Marlatt and Donovan (2005) incorporates social learning into a theory that also calls upon individual resources (such as self-efficacy and ability to enlist alternative strategies to relapse) to help the individual overcome the pressures to relapse.

Cognitive theories

There are a number of theories that explain drug dependence in terms of cognitive constructs. One theory proposes that *self-regulation* is an important factor in the development of drug dependence. Self-regulation has been described as taking "planful action designed to change the course of one's behaviour" (Miller & Brown, 1991, p. 153), the "executive (i.e. non-automatic) capacity to plan, guide and monitor one's behaviour flexibly, according to changing circumstances" (Diaz & Fruhauf, 1991, p. 90). Self-regulation involves planning, taking into account social and physical factors as well as one's own goals, and acting appropriately. Addictive behaviours arise, on this theory, as the result of relying on substance use to maintain a physical and psychological balance.

Self-efficacy is a construct that is also used in social learning theory. Self-efficacy relates to an individual's beliefs about the feasibility of their achieving abstinence. The disease model of addiction, by contrast, assumes that urges to use drugs result from changes in the brain over which the individual has little or no control.

Rational choice theories

One of the central diagnostic features of drug dependence is that addicted individuals have impaired control over their use of the drug. This manifests itself in continued use despite an expressed wish to reduce or stop use of the drug, the use of greater amounts of the drug, or for longer than intended (APA, 1994). By contrast, rational choice theories see behaviour as the result of decision making that weighs the cost and benefits of an action. According to the rational choice theory of addiction, drug taking, and addictive behaviour in general, are explained as the best choice for that individual, given their circumstances. The use of a drug does not reflect loss of control, but it is the outcome of a rational decision.

Decision theories arise from economics, a discipline that sees all behaviour as maximizing "utility" (West, 2006). An individual uses their particular stable individual preferences and physical circumstances to decide whether to use a drug in a particular context or not. Prior experience with the drug, its price, knowledge of its effects (good and/or bad), the individual's concern about these effects, and the social and physical context all contribute to the decision to use or continue to use a drug, and the amount that is used. As West (2006) points out, drug addicts may well express the desire to stop using, but nonetheless continue to use (and thereby appear irrational), because drug use maximizes their utilities in their particular circumstances.

One hypothesis is that this apparent irrationality is explained by human beings' limited ability to consider future benefits – "cognitive myopia" (Herrnstein & Prelec, 1992). According to this view, the choice to use drugs at a particular time may be rational, given the options. Another approach is to argue that when we make these decisions we give a greater weight to the present than the future (Ainslie, 1992; Becker & Murphy, 1988).

Self-medication theories of substance abuse can be seen as a variant of decision models. These theories suggest that addictive or excessive drug taking is a form of rational self-medication that relieves anxiety or excessive stress.

Personality theories

Some theorists argue that some people are more prone to develop addiction because they have an "addictive personality". Longitudinal studies of children have found that, in general, adolescents who are more rebellious and have less conventional social attitudes are more likely to drink, smoke, and use illicit drugs (Institute of Medicine, 1996). This suggests that personality vulnerabilities may lead to later drug use.

Hans Eysenck proposed a psychological *resource model*, in which drug taking develops because a drug fulfils a certain purpose that is related to the individual's personality (Eysenck, 1997). For such people, drug-taking behaviour – or, more specifically, "addiction" – holds benefits even though it also produces negative consequences.

According to Eysenck, there are three major and independent personality dimensions: P (psychoticism), N (neuroticism), and E (extraversion) (Eysenck & Eysenck, 1985). The psychoticism dimension refers to an underlying propensity to functional psychosis, which lies along a continuum from "altruistic" to "schizophrenic" (Eysenck, 1997). Some of the characteristic traits of this dimension are aggression, coldness, egocentricity, impersonality, and impulsivity. The neuroticism dimension refers to a propensity towards emotional lability: moodiness, irritability, and anxiety. Genetic factors are theorized to play an important role in determining these three personality dimensions.

Other genetic theories of addiction exist, such as Cloninger's tridimensional personality theory (Cloninger, 1987). This theory proposes that the three dimensions of novelty seeking, harm avoidance, and reward dependence interact to produce addictive behaviours.

Contextual factors

There are a number of factors in an individual's environment that are strongly related to the risk of substance use and substance use disorders. These are in keeping with the findings of twin studies, which also show a substantial environmental component to addiction vulnerability (Kendler et al., 2007).

In their broad-ranging review of the social determinants of drug use, Spooner and Hetherington (2006) point to environmental factors from conception that affect the likelihood of drug use. Apart from genetic factors and parental drug use in pregnancy, they point to risks in early childhood, such as early-onset behavioural and emotional disturbances and poor school performance. These can be exacerbated by cognitive limitations, poor parenting, and low family socioeconomic status. Carter et al. (2009) also point to the risks associated with these factors as well as the role of disorders of impulse control such as attention-deficit hyperactivity disorder.

Exposure to drugs and drug-using contexts increases the likelihood of drug use and indirectly of developing dependence (Institute of Medicine, 1996; Spooner & Hetherington, 2006). Drug use usually begins with peers, and peer attitudes to drug use are highly predictive of adolescent drug use (Fergusson & Horwood, 1997; Hofler, Lieb, Perkonigg, Schuster, Sonntag, & Wittchen, 1999; Newcomb, Maddahian, & Bentler, 1986), probably because those who use drugs are more likely to affiliate with peers who also use drugs.

People who engage in antisocial behaviour in childhood and adolescence are also more likely to develop substance use problems. Adolescents with conduct disorders are significantly more likely to develop substance use disorders than those without such problems (Cicchetti & Rogosch, 1999; Gittelman, Mannuzza, Shenker, & Bonagura, 1985). In general, the earlier, more varied and more serious a child's antisocial behaviour, the more likely it will continue into adulthood and the more likely that substance misuse will be included among these antisocial behaviours (Costello, Erkanli, Federman, & Angold, 1999; Robins, 1978).

Children or young people with anxiety or depressive symptoms are also more likely to begin substance use at an earlier age, and to develop substance use problems (Cicchetti & Rogosch, 1999; Costello et al., 1999; Loeber, Southamer-Lober, & White, 1999). In these cases the motives for drug use are more likely to be self-medication.

Families have a strong effect on the likelihood that young people will develop substance use problems (Hawkins, Catalano, & Miller, 1992; Lynskey & Hall, 1998). This may occur in a number of ways. First, parents and other family members may model substance use, for example, the children of parents who use drugs are more likely to initiate and become frequent users of alcohol and cannabis (Hawkins et al., 1992). Older brothers' drug use and attitudes towards drug use affect the likelihood of younger brothers using drugs (Brook, Whiteman, Gordon, & Brook, 1988). Second, the children of parents who hold permissive attitudes towards the use of drugs by their children are more likely to use drugs (Hayes, Smart, Toumbourou, & Sanson, 2004). Third, the risk of substance misuse is higher if there is family discord, poor or inconsistent behavioural management by parents, or low levels of bonding within the family (Mak & Kinsella, 1996).

The sociocultural background of a person also affects the likelihood that he or she will develop substance use problems. People who come from lower socioeconomic backgrounds are more likely to have access to and become problematic users of a range of drugs (Anthony, Warner, & Kessler, 1994; Hall, Johnston, & Donnelly, 1999a). So too are those who have completed fewer years of education, or who have performed poorly in school, and young people who have grown up in areas with high rates of crime, where drugs are readily available, and who have associated with delinquent peers (Spooner & Hetherington, 2006).

Synthetic theories of addiction

Theories that attempt to take into account biological as well as psychosocial explanations of behaviour have been called biopsychosocial or synthetic theories. The biopsychosocial model sees "addiction" as a complex behaviour pattern with biological, psychological, sociological, and behavioural components. These include the subjective experience of craving, short-term gratification at the risk of longer-term harm, and rapid change in physical and psychological states. Addictive behaviour is distinguished from other problem behaviours by the individual's pathological involvement in drug use, an intense desire to continue using the drugs, and a lack of control over his or her drug use. The biopsychosocial model of the causes of addictive behaviours forms the basis of many treatment responses to addictions (Marlatt & VandenBos, 1997).

Recently, West (2006) proposed the PRIME theory of addiction (P = plans, R = responses, I = impulses, M = motives and E = evaluations). The PRIME model is a comprehensive approach that attempts to synthesize what we know from research on different theories of addiction, including the important psychobiological changes that occur when people become addicted to drugs. In this theory, the addicted person's motivational system has become dysfunctional, giving an abnormally high priority to using the drug of addiction. The theory states that the motivational system can be distorted by:

1 pre-existing pathologies such as depression, anxiety, low impulse control, poor self-esteem;
2 current abnormalities caused by the addictive behaviour such as sensitization, tolerance, withdrawal, and social impacts such as mood disturbance; and/or
3 pathological environments acting on otherwise normal motivational systems.

The purpose of treatment according to West's framework is to reshape the motivational system.

Summary

Key pathways in the brain are involved in substance use and dependence, and changes occur in the brain's balance and neurotransmitter function after chronic drug use. A variety of factors appear to explain why some people become dependent on drugs. Genetic factors appear to play a part in developing dependence on many of the most commonly used licit and illicit substances. Certain environmental factors also increase the likelihood of problematic substance use, such as economic disadvantage, family conflict, modelling of drug use, or parents' permissive attitudes towards drug use, as well as conduct and emotional problems at an early age.

Psychological approaches to the issue of substance dependence have attempted to explain some of the behavioural and cognitive phenomena thought to underlie problematic substance use. Some theories – such as those proposing a personality type more disposed to addiction, or those characterizing the "rational" addict – have played less of a role in clinical responses to addiction. Learning theories have played more of a role because learning plays an important role in the development and maintenance of substance use problems and learning may also be used to overcome these problems.

Explanations of why some people become dependent on psychoactive substances vary in the level of explanation – biological, psychological, or sociocultural – but all have been supported by empirical research. Comprehensive theories, such as that proposed by West, are providing useful syntheses of these explanations that may assist clinicians in treating addictive disorders.

Alcohol 5

Introduction

Humans have used alcohol for thousands of years for its relaxing and intoxicating effects. In 2004, WHO estimated that around 2 billion people used alcohol and some 76.3 million (3.8%) of drinkers had a diagnosable alcohol disorder. Worldwide, alcohol causes around 20–30% of oesophageal and liver cancers, cirrhosis of the liver, homicide, epilepsy and motor vehicle accidents (WHO, 2004a).

It is not just the volume of alcohol that is consumed but also the patterns of drinking that determine the harms caused by alcohol. In particular, binge drinking or "drinking to get drunk" by young people is a significant contributor to the costs of alcohol to our society. In 2003, it was estimated that alcohol caused 3.8% of deaths worldwide and 4.6% of disability-adjusted life years (DALYs). The DALYs attributable to alcohol were far greater among men (6.5%) than women (1.3%), and unintentional injuries accounted for a quarter of these DALYs in both sexes. The costs of alcohol use to society average around 2.1% of gross domestic product in high- and middle-income countries (Rehm et al., 2009). A recent report from Australia, where over 80% of adults regularly use alcohol, has estimated that the total tangible and intangible costs, including costs to others affected by an individual's drinking, is around $36 billion (Laslett et al., 2010).

Alcohol is used widely throughout the world, and thus, alcohol use disorders are among the most prevalent disorders diagnosed in community surveys of mental disorders. Many people with these disorders also have comorbid anxiety and depressive disorders (Teesson et al., 2010). For those who present to treatment services it is important that best evidence-based practices are in place.

Prevention

Large numbers of adolescents drink above safe drinking limits and much effort has been put into developing strategies to help prevent alcohol misuse in young people. These have been of both a psychological and educational nature. In a large-scale systematic review, Foxcroft, Ireland, Lowe, and Breen (2002) considered the effectiveness of interventions for prevention over the short term (less than 1 year), medium term (1–3 years), and long term (greater than 3 years). They identified 56 programmes of which 20 were found to be ineffective. The review also found a culturally focused skills-training approach that showed promise but needed proper evaluation (Schinke, Tepavac, & Cole, 2000).

Prevention is the focus of considerable research activity and recently a brief personality-targeted substance use preventive intervention for high-risk adolescents aged 14–15 years has been shown to be effective. *Preventure* is the first and only targeted school-based alcohol and illicit drug prevention programme that has been shown to prevent growth in alcohol and substance misuse in Canada and the UK (Conrod, Castellanos, & Strang, 2010). Universal computer-delivered interventions have also shown considerable promise. The *Climate* programme is based on an effective harm-minimization approach to prevention and uses cartoon storylines to engage and maintain student interest (Newton, Andrews, Teesson, & Vogl, 2009b; Newton, Vogl, Teesson, & Andrews, 2009a; Vogl, Teesson, Andrews, Dillon, & Steadman, 2009). This is a growing area of research activity.

Assessment

Assessment is an important first stage in intervention and treatment for alcohol problems, and involves a review of the quantity and frequency of alcohol use and the health and social consequences of drinking. Two important roles of the assessment are to provide feedback to the individual on his or her alcohol use and to develop a rapport between the therapist and the individual. The aim of assessment is to:

- identify why the individual continues to drink at harmful levels;
- identify any other comorbid disorders or problems (identify harms);

- highlight the areas that require intervention (e.g., alcohol consumption patterns, depression) to enable goals to be set and a management plan to be devised; and
- identify a baseline against which improvement or deterioration can be measured.

Assessment can range from brief screening interviews by general healthcare workers, which may lead to early intervention, to in-depth assessment of a broad range of psychosocial functions in order to formulate and evaluate treatment for more serious problems.

Standardized methods of screening for *excessive drinking* include the use of clinical examinations, testing for biological markers, and the use of standardized questionnaires. Standard clinical examinations, which involve identifying physical signs of excessive alcohol consumption, such as bloodshot eyes and coating of the tongue, have been found to be accurate for detecting alcohol dependence but are not sensitive enough to detect signs of hazardous, non-dependent drinking (Mattick & Jarvis, 1993). The most widely used biological marker for alcohol abuse is serum gamma glutamyltransferase (GGT), a liver enzyme that is elevated in 55–80% of people with alcohol disorders.

The Alcohol Use Disorders Identification Test (AUDIT, Saunders, Aasland, Babor, de le Fuente, & Grant, 1993; Babor, Higgens-Biddle, Saunders, & Montiero, 2001; see Table 5.1) was developed as a screen for alcohol misuse in medical settings in a range of countries and populations. It is useful for screening both adults and adolescents (Dawe, Loxton, Hides, Kavanagh, & Mattick, 2002). It is particularly effective in identifying low-level hazardous drinking. It is less useful in identifying drinking problems among elderly people.

A shortened 3-item version of the AUDIT has been developed (AUDIT-C; see Table 5.2), and recent research indicates that it displays excellent psychometric properties across all age groups, gender and US ethnic groups, and in the presence of comorbid psychiatric disorders (Dawson, Grant, & Stinson, 2005a; Dawson, Grant, Stinson, & Zhou, 2005b; Frank et al., 2008; Gomez et al., 2006). A score of greater than two or three in women and four in men is recommended as a cut-off to indicate alcohol misuse, while a score of five or more for both men and women should be used as a cut-off to indicate a probable alcohol use disorder (Bradley, DeBenedetti, Volk, Williams, Frank, & Kivlahan, 2007). The AUDIT-C provides a score that can be used to monitor the primary care patient's risk over time. Its brevity should recommend it to busy primary care physicians.

TABLE 5.1

Alcohol Use Disorders Identification Test (AUDIT)

Circle the number that comes closest to your answer.

1 How often do you have a drink containing alcohol?

(0) Never   (1) Monthly or   (2) 2–4 times a   (3) 2–3 times a   (4) 4 or more
              less   month   week   times a week

2 How many drinks containing alcohol do you have on a typical day when you are drinking?

(0) 1 or 2   (1) 3 or 4   (2) 5 or 6   (3) 7 to 9   (4) 10 or more

3 How often do you have six or more drinks on one occasion?

(0) Never   (1) Less than   (2) Monthly   (3) Weekly   (4) Daily or
              monthly   almost daily

4 How often during the last year have you found that you were not able to stop drinking once you had started?

(0) Never   (1) Less than   (2) Monthly   (3) Weekly   (4) Daily or
              monthly   almost daily

5 How often during the last year have you failed to do what was normally expected from you because of drinking?

(0) Never   (1) Less than   (2) Monthly   (3) Weekly   (4) Daily or
              monthly   almost daily

6 How often during the last year have you needed a first drink in the morning to get yourself going after a heavy drinking session?

(0) Never   (1) Less than   (2) Monthly   (3) Weekly   (4) Daily or
              monthly   almost daily

7 How often during the last year have you had a feeling of guilt or remorse after drinking?

(0) Never   (1) Less than   (2) Monthly   (3) Weekly   (4) Daily or
              monthly   almost daily

8 How often during the last year have you been unable to remember what happened the night before because you had been drinking?

(0) Never   (1) Less than   (2) Monthly   (3) Weekly   (4) Daily or
              monthly   almost daily

9 Have you or someone else been injured as a result of your drinking?

(0) No   (2) Yes, but not in   (4) Yes, during
                              the last year   the last year

10 Has a relative or friend or a doctor or other health care worker been concerned about your drinking or suggested you cut down?

(0) No   (2) Yes, but not in   (4) Yes, during
                              the last year   the last year

© World Health Organization (2001), reproduced with permission.

TABLE 5.2

AUDIT-C Screening Questionnaire

1 How often do you have a drink containing alcohol?

Never (0 points)	Monthly or less (1 points)	2–4 times a month (2 points)	2–3 times a week (3 points)	4 or more times a week (4 points)

2 How many drinks containing alcohol do you have on a typical day when you are drinking?

1 or 2 (0 points)	3 or 4 (1 points)	5 or 6 (2 points)	7 to 9 (3 points)	10 or more (4 points)

3 How often do you have six or more drinks on one occasion?

Never (0 points)	Less than monthly (1 points)	Monthly (2 points)	Weekly (3 points)	Daily or almost daily (4 points)

© World Health Organization (2001), reproduced with permission.

The AUDIT-C still has to be scored and, if time is constrained, then experts recommend that a single question measuring episodic heavy drinking can be used as an initial screen (National Institute on Alcohol Abuse and Alcoholism and National Institutes of Health, 2005). Question 3 in AUDIT can be used with a cut-off of monthly or more as indicative of risky drinking.

One of the most widely used instruments for assessing the *severity of alcohol dependence* is the Severity of Alcohol Dependence Questionnaire (SADQ, Stockwell, Sitharthan, McGrath, & Lang, 1994). This 20-item instrument (with a maximum score of 60) has excellent psychometric properties and emphasizes symptoms of physical dependence. Scores lower than or equal to 20 indicate low dependence; scores between 21 and 30 indicate moderate dependence; and a score of 30 indicates severe dependence (Stockwell, Murphy, & Hodgson, 1983).

The Short Alcohol Dependence Data Questionnaire (SADDQ, Raistrick, Dunbar, & Davidson, 1983) is similar to the SADQ, but focuses less on physical symptoms of alcohol dependence, such as withdrawal symptoms, and more emphasis on psychological elements of dependence, such as behavioural and subjective manifestations. The 24-item Alcohol Dependence Scale (ADS, Skinner & Horn, 1984) is a widely used questionnaire with good reliability and validity.

Self-efficacy relates to an individual's confidence in being able to drink moderately. It has been recognized as an important therapeutic construct in alcohol treatment. The Controlled Drinking Situational Confidence Questionnaire (Sitharthan & Kavanagh, 1991) provides a very useful measure of self-efficacy by asking the client to rate his or her confidence in being able to drink moderately.

Physical well-being – as indicated by liver function, blood pressure, withdrawal symptoms, and organic brain damage – should be included in the overall assessment, and the results may prove useful in counselling against continued hazardous drinking.

Cognitive dysfunction should also be assessed by neuropsychological tests. Excessive tremor in the hands and fingers (and even the tongue), staggering gait, and numbness in the fingers and toes also indicate damage to the central nervous system. Such signs should be carefully checked, especially in severe long-term drinkers. The issue will often arise as to whether an individual with an alcohol problem is suffering from brain damage. The diagnosis of lesser degrees of damage is often quite difficult, but one of the most common presentations is alcohol dementia. The individual with alcohol dementia will typically give a history of many years of drinking and may present as the example below:

> A young man, aged 30 years, had been drinking heavily for five years. He reported that his wife complained about his irritability and impaired concentration. His performance as a store manager had recently been reviewed and his boss's appraisal was that his work performance was deteriorating.

Comorbid drug and mental disorders are common among alcohol-dependent persons seeking treatment. They can influence the course and severity of the disorder and the treatment process and their presence should be assessed. Brief screeners can be useful in this context such as the Depression Anxiety Stress Scale (DASS, Lovibond & Lovibond, 1995); Kessler's 10 Psychological Distress Scale (K10, Kessler, 1996); Cannabis Problems Questionnaire (Copeland, Gilmour, Gates, & Swift, 2005); and a psychosis screener (Degenhardt, Hall, Korten, & Jablensky, 2005).

> A single woman, aged 25 years, had been drinking excessively for 5 years. She attended her GP's surgery complaining that she was unable to get out of bed in the

morning and felt that she was no good and that the world might as well be rid of her.

The clinician should not only assess her alcohol use but also the severity of her symptoms of depression.

Family issues may have an important bearing on treatment compliance and outcome. Such factors include how the individual's drinking affects family relations, the quality of family relations in general, the presence of violence and abuse, and the commitment of the family to the rehabilitation of the individual. The Alcohol Problems Questionnaire provides an appraisal of family, occupational, and global alcohol-related problems (Williams & Drummond, 1994).

Interventions

Public health interventions

Not all problems with alcohol require individual treatment, and some alcohol problems in the community may be better modified in other ways. Public health policies that reduce the availability and increase the price of alcohol may reduce the prevalence of alcohol abuse and dependence. Public education about the risks of alcohol dependence may prevent the more prevalent and less severe alcohol use disorders, while advice on self-help strategies can obviate the need for professional assistance in a substantial proportion of less severe cases.

A major development in the prevention of alcoholism and alcohol-related health problems has been the adoption of a public health perspective that shifts attention away from an exclusive focus on the dependent drinker to consider the full spectrum of problems caused by alcohol (e.g., road traffic accidents, lost productivity, violence, and diseases such as cancer, liver cirrhosis, brain damage, and heart disease (Edwards et al., 1994)). An important consequence of this perspective is the recognition that the prevalence of alcohol-related problems in the community can best be reduced by decreasing the alcohol consumption of a much larger proportion of the population than the minority of those with more severe problems.

The lack of popular and political support for policies that increase the price of alcohol or reduce its availability (Flaherty, Homel, & Hall, 1991) has encouraged a search for other approaches to reduce the public health impact of alcohol use. Foremost among these has been the public education of drinkers about the risks of alcohol use. This has been especially prominent in Australia, where a combination of education about the maximum number of standard drinks that can be consumed before driving and random breath testing have reduced overall road fatalities and the proportion of fatalities in which the driver had a blood alcohol level above the prescribed limit (0.05%). These campaigns enjoy widespread public support and have probably also helped to reduce consumption by providing an excuse for drinkers to moderate their consumption (Homel, 1989).

Collins and Lapsley (2008a) analysed Australian data on the social costs of alcohol and concluded that the following public health interventions would be effective in cutting these costs even further:

1 higher alcohol taxation, including differential tax rates on forms of alcohol that are particularly subject to abuse;
2 partial or complete bans on the advertising and promotion of alcohol;
3 measures to reduce drink driving – more intensive enforcement of random breath testing and lowering the legal blood alcohol concentration (BAC) level;
4 brief interventions by primary care physicians to reduce hazardous alcohol consumption;
5 control of drinking environments;
6 alcohol ignition locks on vehicles driven by convicted drink-driving offenders;
7 guidelines for low-risk drinking; and
8 standard drinks labelling and health warnings on drinks containers (Collins & Lapsley, 2008a, pp. ix–x).

They found that implementing the first four of these measures would reduce the social costs of alcohol by around a half.

Brief interventions

People presenting for medical treatment can be screened for hazardous alcohol use and alcohol-related problems, and those identified as drinking at hazardous levels can be advised to reduce or stop consumption and be given advice on simple ways to achieve these goals (Heather & Tebbutt, 1989). Such brief interventions were first promoted by early researchers in the tobacco-smoking cessation field (Russell & Bigler, 1979). They found that 5-minute opportunistic interventions by GPs, when delivered to thousands of patients who had come to consult about another health matter, had a larger impact on quit rates in the community than intensive interventions delivered to a select few who requested help.

Extending this research to alcohol use disorders, Heather (1998) found that interventions ranging from 5 minutes to 1 hour, delivered either opportunistically or on request, reduced drinking among problem drinkers with mild dependence. This included occasional binge drinkers, as well as steady drinkers who wanted help to reduce their intake. The interventions included: information on safe drinking limits; information about the harmful effects of alcohol; suggestions on useful techniques to cut down; and advice on how to self-monitor their daily alcohol intake.

Miller and Marlatt (1984) in the USA developed a Comprehensive Drinker Profile (CDP) that allowed a therapist to provide a standardized assessment. Appropriate feedback about the likely harm arising from the client's drinking is used to put the client in a position to decide what to do about the problem. The CDP is designed to boost client motivation to make changes, and is therefore a particularly effective form of brief intervention. Updated and shorter versions of this profile (the Brief Drinker Profile and the Briefer Drinker Profile) are freely available for download from the web.

A seminal study on brief interventions for alcohol misuse was carried out by the WHO Brief Intervention Study Group (1996). This was a cross-national, randomized clinical trial comparing a no-treatment control condition with two treatment conditions: 5 minutes of advice or 20 minutes of brief counselling. The initial sample consisted of 1,260 men and 399 women with no history of alcohol dependence who were identified as being at risk of alcohol-related problems. The sample was taken from eight countries: Australia, Kenya, Mexico, Norway, the UK, Russia, the USA and Zimbabwe. Subjects were followed up 9 months later; 75% of the sample was interviewed at follow-up and it was assumed for purposes of analysis that those not available for follow-up continued to drink at baseline levels. Significant improvements were found for males in both treatment groups compared with the control group, but there was no difference between the two treatments. Overall treatment led to a 17% reduction in average daily consumption and a 10% reduction in intensity of drinking and this was consistent between countries. These findings were not due to a few patients achieving abstinence but were distributed across many patients who reduced their drinking by small but meaningful amounts. This indicates that moderate drinking can be achieved by a substantial proportion of heavy drinkers.

A recent Cochrane Review has corroborated these findings and those of the many studies that have been carried out in this area (Kaner et al., 2007). The review demonstrated that brief interventions to reduce alcohol consumption in primary care patients, who were not seeking treatment for alcohol problems, significantly reduce drinking outcomes at 1-year follow-up. It also confirmed (a) that these findings apply to men but not women; and (b) that duration of the counselling session had little impact on drinking outcomes.

One criticism of this research is that brief interventions represent a range of treatments that vary in length and content. For example, the Cochrane Review (Kaner et al., 2007, p. 10) described the included brief interventions as follows: "Participants received any or all of: motivational interviews; cognitive behavioural therapy; self-completed action plans; leaflets, either on general health issues or specifically about alcohol; requests to keep drinking diaries; written personalised feedback; follow-up telephone counselling; and exercises to complete at home" and "The number of sessions ranged from one to five, individual sessions varied from 1 to 50 minutes, while total intervention exposure time ranged from a mean of 7.5 minutes to 60 minutes. Professionals administering the intervention were general practitioners, nurse practitioners or psychologists." Despite this heterogeneity, the review could conclude that, overall, brief serendipitous interventions had significant impacts on drinking outcomes – among men. They conclude that further research is needed to ascertain the most effective components of the interventions, as well as to determine which brief interventions, if any, can be best applied to women.

In order to encourage best practice in interventions in primary care for alcohol use disorders, the National Institute on Alcohol Abuse and Alcoholism and National Institutes of Health (2005) in the USA have prepared guidelines that are available for download from their website.

Two recent large-scale reviews found inconclusive evidence on the efficacy of opportunistic brief interventions in hospital settings (Emmen, Schippers, Bleijenberg, & Wollersheim, 2004; McQueen, Howe, Allan, & Mains, 2009). Both reviews concluded that brief interventions may be effective in this population, but further research was required. A similar conclusion was drawn in a systematic review of brief interventions in the workplace (Webb, Shakeshaft, Sanson-Fisher, & Havard, 2009).

Another large-scale review examined research on *social norms interventions* in US college students (Moreira, Smith, & Foxcroft, 2009).

These interventions address the students' perceptions and beliefs about what is normal drinking behaviour, on the assumption that most students have an exaggerated view of how much their fellow students drink. The interventions inform the individual about drinking norms among their peers and compare the individual's drinking with these norms. These interventions may also include information on risks associated with heavy drinking as well as brief counselling, individual or group. Moreira and colleagues (2009) found that use of social norm comparisons in individual face-to-face settings or through the internet, reduced alcohol misuse. They found no evidence that mailed or group interventions were any better than standard (control) interventions.

Detoxification

Detoxification is the removal of a drug from the body. It involves assisting the individual to recover from the effects of chronic intoxication so that withdrawal symptoms are minimized. The severity of alcohol withdrawal depends on such factors as level and duration of use, accompanying drug use, the general health and nutritional state of the person, and the detoxification setting (Mattick & Jarvis, 1993). Withdrawal or detoxification from alcohol can be life threatening.

Detoxification itself can be medicated or unmedicated. Over recent decades, benzodiazapines have been considered most effective in assisting this process (Assanangkornchai & Srisurapanont, 2007). Recently anticonvulsants such as carbamazepine and topiramate have been trialled with generally positive findings in comparison to no-drug and benzodiazepine controls. Again more research is needed (Ait-Daoud, Malcolm, & Johnson, 2006; Minozzi, Amato, Vecchi, & Davoli, 2010). Similarly Leone and colleagues (Leone, Vigna-Taglianti, Avanzi, Brambilla, & Faggiano, 2010), in a recent Cochrane Review, found generally positive findings for the use of gamma-hydroxy-butyric acid (GHB) to prevent and suppress withdrawal symptoms. The authors conclude that more trials of this drug are warranted as it is the only medication demonstrated to reduce craving during alcohol withdrawal.

Detoxification can be home-based or inpatient. Withdrawal at home may be appropriate when a person is considered likely to suffer mild to moderate withdrawal, is not in need of medication, and has no medical or psychiatric history that may complicate the process (Hayashida et al., 1989). Even in cases of severe and medicated withdrawal, medication may be administered at home where social conditions permit (Stockwell et al., 1991). Adding a psychological intervention to home detoxification can significantly improve outcomes in a cost-effective way (Alwyn, John, Hodgson, & Phillips, 2004). Inpatient detoxification is warranted when the severity of dependence (and thus likely complications) is high, or where there are no supportive relatives or friends to assist with home monitoring. Purpose-built detoxification units rather than acute medical wards provide the best conditions for inpatient withdrawal (Alterman, Hayashida, & O'Brien, 1988; Pedersen, 1986).

Detoxification is often confused with treatment. Mattick and Hall (1996) point out that, although detoxification is an important first step in treatment for those addicted, especially where the degree of dependence is great, it is not a treatment in its own right. People who have undergone detoxification programmes are equally as likely to relapse as those who have not. Mattick and Hall note that the benefits of detoxification in general arise because of (1) the opportunity it provides for a change in lifestyle with the help of other interventions and (2) the harm reduction effects where continued heavy alcohol usage could lead to serious complications, including death.

Treatment goal: Abstinence or moderation

The controlled drinking debate is one of the great debates in the addictions. Research suggests that less dependent drinkers may achieve controlled drinking, whereas severely dependent drinkers should aim at abstinence (Mattick & Jarvis, 1993). Sobell and Sobell (1995) argue that irrespective of the stated treatment goals or the amount of drinking skills training, the most likely positive outcome of treatment for low-dependence drinkers is controlled drinking, while for high dependence drinkers, it is abstinence. They point out that background factors, such as lack of social support and poor vocational history, may be more important in deciding treatment aims than level of dependence.

There has been much interest and controversy about moderation as a legitimate treatment goal for alcohol dependence because it directly conflicts with the tenets of Alcoholics Anonymous (AA) that holds that no "alcoholic" is able to moderate his or her consumption of alcohol for any length of time. Abstinence, according to AA, is the only defensible and achievable goal for persons who are alcohol dependent.

The earliest work in this area was conducted by Davies (1962) working with hospitalized patients in the UK. He found in a 10-year follow-up that a substantial proportion of the cohort had returned to drinking moderately. Sobell and Sobell (1995) followed this preliminary research with one of the first randomized controlled trials in the alcohol treatment literature. They found that problem drinkers were just as likely to master controlled drinking as those who trained in abstinence techniques. Research suggests that those who have a dependence on alcohol that is mild to moderate (which can be measured by the Severity of Alcohol Dependence Questionnaire), have good means of social support, and have a stable psychosocial profile are more likely to succeed with controlled drinking (Heather & Robertson, 1983). More recently, Maisto, Clifford, Stout, and Davis (2007) have confirmed that controlled drinking may be the most suitable goal for alcohol treatment for some individuals. Perhaps the foremost indicator of outcome of a controlled drinking intervention is the individual's desire to become a safe drinker.

Psychosocial interventions

A range of psychosocial interventions has been found to be effective in treating alcohol dependence. These are often clearly described in manuals that ensure effective procedures are followed. In their large-scale review, Miller and Wilbourne (2002, p. 265) found that, apart from brief interventions, the strongest evidence of efficacy among psychosocial interventions was for "social skills training, the community reinforcement approach, behavior contracting, behavioral marital therapy, and case management". They also found that the "least supported were methods designed to educate, confront, shock, or foster insight regarding the nature and causes of alcoholism" (p. 265).

Cognitive behavioural therapy

Cognitive behavioural therapy (CBT) is based on social learning theory and assumes alcohol abuse stems from negative life experiences. Treatment aims to address skills deficits, and improve coping with situations where relapse is likely to occur. CBT aims to teach individuals how to control their responses to their environment through improving social, coping, and problem-solving skills. It is widely agreed that CBT is an important and effective treatment for abuse of alcohol (Assanangkornchai & Srisurapanont, 2007; Magill & Ray, 2009; Saitz, 2007). It appears to be most effective for individuals who have less severe alcohol-related problems and have had a shorter duration of drinking problems.

Social skills training is the CBT approach that has some of the strongest evidence of outcome efficacy (Monti & Rohsenow, 1999). In this intervention the client learns effective coping skills to manage problems with personal (thoughts, emotions) and social (interpersonal communication, stress, conflict) situations. For many problem drinkers, alcohol is the preferred means of coping with many difficult or threatening situations. Thus, training in social skills helps problem drinkers to overcome many of the major triggers for relapse. The evidence for this approach has been consistently strong, and it has also proved to be a popular form of intervention with both therapists and clients. This style of intervention, like all CBT approaches, has the advantage that it can be delivered in either group or individual format.

CBT is an effective treatment procedure that appears to work best with non-dependent problem drinkers. It can be delivered in various formats (face to face, internet, telephone, and mail), and serves as an important adjuvant therapy for pharmacological interventions.

Motivational enhancement therapy

Motivational enhancement therapy (MET), also known as Motivational interviewing (MI), uses motivational strategies that aim to mobilize the individual's own resources rather than specifying a particular path to recovery. Miller and Rollnick (2002, p. 25) defined MI as "a client-centered, directive method for enhancing intrinsic motivation to change by exploring and resolving ambivalence". They outline the following as the key principles of MET:

1 emphasize the individual's present interests and problems;
2 selectively respond to the client's speech in a way that resolves ambivalence and motivates the person to change;
3 treat it as a method of communication rather than a set of techniques;
4 focus on intrinsic motivation for change; and
5 within this approach, change occurs because of its relevance to the person's own values.

The basic therapeutic strategies of MET are to express empathy, develop discrepancy, avoid argumentation, roll with resistance, and support self-efficacy (Miller & Rollnick, 1991).

There are several strategies that can be incorporated into MET for alcohol problems, one of which is exploring the pros and cons of continuing alcohol misuse. This strategy is designed to help the individual to express concern about alcohol use. The individual is prompted to consider the situation by listing the "good things" (PROS) and "less good things" (CONS) about alcohol use.

Sue, 26 years old, was in treatment for problems with alcohol. She was drinking more than 10 standard drinks a day. She filled out the following list early in her treatment:

PROS and CONS ratings for Sue:

PROS	CONS
1. Relaxation	1. Cost of drinks
2. Drinking with friends	2. Hangovers and headaches
3. Helps me forget things	3. Guilt

Another key strategy is to help the client to think about his or her past life and compare this with how things seem now. The life satisfaction strategy uses the discrepancy between how things are and how they were, or could be. The individual is asked "When you were (age), what did you think you would be doing now?" It is then possible to note discrepancies between past expectations and the current situation and explore the link between drug and alcohol use and goals and aspirations.

MET has demonstrated efficacy as a standalone treatment and in combination with other effective strategies. A meta-analysis of its effectiveness (Vasilaki, Hosier, & Cox, 2006, p. 328) concluded that it is effective in reducing alcohol consumption. It also found that it is probably more effective in younger adults who are heavy drinkers than with older drinkers with more severe drinking problems.

Family and marital therapy

The purpose of family and marital therapy (FMT) is to engage significant others in the rehabilitation of individuals who abuse alcohol. Various types of family therapy have been trialled: systems, interactional, behavioural, and spouse-directed (Mattick & Jarvis, 1993). The contingency-based community reinforcement approach (CRA), developed by Azrin and colleagues (Azrin, Acierno, Kogan, Donohue, Besalel, & McMahon, 1996), also engages those close to the affected person in a behaviourally oriented approach to treatment. CRA was developed as an intensive and broad-ranging approach that addresses community reinforcers both within and outside the family to encourage interests and activities that support abstinence. Since CRA involves close family members, it falls within the domain of behavioural family and marital approaches. A recent systematic review (Roozen, Boulogne, van Tulder, van den Brink, De Jong, & Kerkhof, 2004) found that there was some support for the efficacy of CRA in the treatment of drug and alcohol problems: with or without pharmacotherapy or contingency management.

In a comprehensive review of the alcohol treatment outcome literature, Mattick and Jarvis (1993) found that behavioural marital therapy (BMT) was more effective than no treatment at all, but was no more effective than individual alcohol counselling or brief advice and follow-up. Two recent studies (McCrady, Epstein, Cook, Jensen, & Hildebrandt, 2009; Vedel, Emmelkamp, & Schippers, 2008) compared CBT and BMT in community settings and found that both improved alcohol outcomes and there was no difference in outcomes between the two methods. There was some evidence that BMT improved the marital relationship. Given that BMT tends to involve longer sessions (usually double the time) and is thus considerably more costly, there is little evidence at this stage that inclusion of the spouse or significant others in treatment is any more effective than individual treatment.

Cue exposure

Exposure to alcohol cues (objects, people, or situations associated with drinking) while not drinking has been hypothesized to decrease craving and increase self-efficacy and, in turn, improve long-term drinking outcomes. In small individual studies, cue exposure has been found to be more effective than a relaxation control (Drummond & Glautier, 1994; Rohsenow et al., 2001) and as effective as CBT for patients with moderate severity alcohol dependence (Loeber, Croissant, Heinz, Mann, & Flor, 2006). More research is required to confirm the value of this type of intervention and to identify the patients for whom it is likely to be most effective (Szegedi, Lorch, Scheurich, Ruppe, Hautzinger, & Wetzel, 2000).

Alcoholics Anonymous

Alcoholics Anonymous (AA) is the oldest and most widely utilized treatment intervention for alcohol dependence. AA and other 12-step therapies assume that substance dependence is a spiritual and a medical disease. Despite its longevity and public profile there has been little research on its efficacy. This arises in part from one of the tenets of the organization, which holds that all members shall remain anonymous, and so discourages collection of any personal details. A recent Cochrane Review found no evidence that AA or other 12-step approaches were more effective than other psychosocial interventions (Ferri, Amato, & Davoli, 2006).

The Project MATCH Research Group (1997) provided some evidence that a treatment programme that introduced alcohol-dependent patients to the teachings of AA (12-step facilitation therapy or TSF) produced equivalent 12-month drinking outcomes to CBT and MET. The 3-year follow-up showed marginally better outcomes in the TSF group reflecting greater rates of attendance at 12-step meetings. However, the manualized TSF approach tested in this study cannot be considered equivalent to what happens in a typical AA meeting. Rather than providing evidence of efficacy of AA, this research lends support to the notion that many individual psycho-social interventions have equivalent efficacy. The issue is to identify what it is in these therapies that makes them effective.

Mattick and Jarvis (1993) concluded that AA provides an accessible avenue for self-help and ongoing social support for those who choose abstinence as their goal, but there is no convincing evidence that AA alone is effective. This conclusion still holds today (Ferri et al., 2006).

Matching client to psychosocial treatment

Project MATCH (1997) was one of the largest treatment outcome studies in alcohol research. Treatment strategies, client-matching variables, and the specific hypotheses for the study were based on theoretical considerations and prior empirical findings. Three treatment strategies were compared: CBT, MET, and TSF, which aimed to foster participation in the fellowship activities of AA. The study examined after the event whether clients with different characteristics responded differently to the three treatments.

There were substantial positive changes in percent days abstinent and average number of drinks per drinking day in both aftercare and outpatient subjects at the 12-month follow-up. There were no consistent and clinically meaningful differences between the three treatments in outcome at 12 months in either the aftercare or outpatient groups. The study found little support for the matching hypothesis, in that response to the three treatments did not depend on any of the patient characteristics assessed.

These findings were corroborated more recently in the UK (UKATT Research Team, 2008), which matched clients to two treatments: MET and social behaviour and network therapy, the latter focusing on developing social support for a positive change in drinking behaviour. This study also found no evidence that client–treatment matching on the basis of client attributes improved outcomes of treatment for alcohol problems.

Stepped care

Many experts suggest that a stepped care approach to alcohol treatment is the most cost effective. This approach involves using minimal intervention initially and only using more intensive interventions if the initial intervention does not have the desired effect. A recent large study compared the effectiveness and cost-effectiveness of a stepped care approach to a minimal intervention (Drummond et al., 2009). The stepped care approach consisted of three successive steps:

1 a single session of behaviour change counselling delivered by a practice nurse;
2 four 50-minute sessions of motivational enhancement therapy delivered by a trained alcohol counsellor; and
3 referral to a community alcohol treatment agency.

The control or minimal intervention consisted of 5 minutes of minimal intervention delivered by a practice nurse. The study found that the stepped care approach produced equivalent or better outcomes than the brief intervention and was more cost-effective.

Other options for a stepped care approach, which show considerable promise, employ the internet and/or telephone contact.

Telephone/internet/mail-based interventions

Since not all clients respond well to face-to-face interventions, other means of delivering cost-effective treatments have been explored, including: telephone, mail and web-based interventions. Two recent reviews conclude that web-based interventions (e-therapy) for alcohol problems, although having high drop-out rates, have positive impacts on drinking outcomes (Elliott, Carey, & Bolles, 2008; Vernon, 2010). e-therapy may more effectively reach some sub-populations than do face-to-face therapies, for example women, higher-educated people, employed people and elderly people (Postel, de Jong, & de Haan, 2005). Research also shows that web-based interventions are independently effective within population sub-groups (Riper,

Kramer, Keuken, Smit, Schippers, & Cuijpers, 2008). Because of this broad-based effectiveness, use of e-therapy as the first step in a stepped care approach is a recommended cost-effective option.

A study by Brown and colleagues (Brown, Saunders, Bobula, Mundt, & Koch, 2007) found that a six-session telephone and mail intervention was more effective than a pamphlet in reducing drinking in non-treatment seeking men with alcohol disorders. A large-scale study in Germany by Bischof and colleagues (Bischof, Grothues, Reinhardt, Meyer, John, & Rumpf, 2008) provided support for both a stepped care and combined computer–telephone-based approach. A stepped care approach using a computerized intervention as a first step and telephone follow-up had equivalent drinking outcomes and significantly better cost outcomes than a fixed computer–telephone intervention. Both interventions had superior outcomes to an untreated control group.

Another study using Swedish University students (Johnsson & Berglund, 2006) found that a mailed brief intervention was equally as effective as a 10-hour face-to-face CBT intervention. Thus, interventions by mail and telephone, which are far less costly than face-to-face interventions, show promise as treatments for at-risk drinking. Along with computerized interventions, they should be considered as feasible first steps in a stepped care approach to treatment of alcohol problems in the community.

Pharmacotherapies

There are a limited number of drugs that can be used to assist people with alcohol problems to become and remain abstinent. One of the first pharmacotherapies was disulfiram (marketed as Antabuse). This medicine was classed as an "antidipsotropic". It inhibits the enzyme that catalyses the breakdown of acetaldehyde in the blood. When alcohol is used acetaldehyde levels rise causing nausea, vomiting, and shortness of breath. It has proved useful for problem drinkers who are highly motivated towards abstinence but has had limited success because many drinkers either discontinue their medication, or deliberately miss doses in order to drink.

Schuckit (1996), in his review of this area, concluded that the clinical effectiveness of disulfiram is modest at best, and that the use of this treatment needs to be carefully considered in view of the risks of side effects such as peripheral neuropathy and hepatitis. This concern was reiterated in a recent review by Saitz (2007). More recent research suggests it may have an important place in the treatment of clients who are well motivated and have supplementary psychotherapy or counselling for their problem.

An improved understanding of brain neurobiology over recent decades has led to the development of new pharmacological treatments to assist in relapse prevention. Approximately 50% of people who are alcohol dependent relapse within 3 months of treatment. Newer medications used to reduce relapse into heavy drinking include acamprosate and naltrexone (oral and long acting). Psychosocial support during pharmacotherapy for alcohol dependence is considered best practice for these newer medications (Weiss & Kueppenbender, 2006).

A recent Cochrane Review of the efficacy of the opioid antagonists, naltrexone and nalmefene in preventing relapse in people with alcohol dependence found that short-term (up to 3 months) treatment with naltrexone is an effective intervention. There was insufficient evidence on nalmefene to make any final recommendations (Rösner, Hackle-Herrwerth, Leucht, Vecchi, Srisurapanont, & Soyka, 2010). Acamprosate, which is thought to act on the brain pathways affected by alcohol misuse, has been found to be an effective treatment for alcohol disorders. However, it should not be taken by people with kidney problems or who have an allergy to the drug. Rates of abstinence have been found to be higher with acamprosate than placebo, as have percent days abstinent and time to first drink (Singleton, Bumpstead, O'Brien, Lee, & Meltzer, 2003).

The neurobiology of anticonvulsants has encouraged research on the use of this class of medication to treat relapse. Topiramate has shown particular promise in recent studies, showing efficacy for drinking outcomes and quality of life, as well as general safety (Olmsted & Kockler, 2008). Other anticonvulsants that are less well researched but have shown positive findings are oxcarbazepine and divalproex. More research is required before any anticonvulsants can be considered a first-line pharmacotherapy for alcohol dependence.

Dopaminergic agents such as tiapride and olanzapine have been found to reduce craving and alcohol consumption in humans in laboratory settings but large-scale randomised trials are yet to be completed on these drugs. The GABA-B receptor agonist baclofen has been studied in a few placebo-controlled trials with equivocal findings (Garbutt, 2009).

A Cochrane Review by Leone and colleagues (2010) concluded that the anaesthetic sedative GHB was superior to naltrexone and disulfiram in maintaining abstinence and was more effective in reducing craving than placebo and disulfiram. Side effects were considered limited and manageable and did not differ significantly from benzodiazepines, naltrexone, or disulfiram. The most common side effect of GHB was dizziness and vertigo (around 20% where stated in trials). Given that dependence and withdrawal on GHB is largely a problem among polydrug abusers or previous abusers, the authors conclude that GHB should be avoided for this group of patients. Further studies are needed to establish optimal dose schedules.

Treating complex clients (comorbidity)

People presenting for treatment for their alcohol problems can have other physical, psychiatric, or drug use problems, especially comorbid anxiety and depressive disorders. The presence of any comorbidity means the patient is more difficult to treat and has poorer treatment outcomes. Patients with alcohol and other drug problems comorbid with the less common but more severe psychiatric disorders such as schizophrenia and bipolar disorder are more likely to be found in the psychiatric services. The presence of alcohol and other drug problems in these patients means that they will remain unwell for longer periods and be admitted more often to hospital and psychiatric care.

In his review of the research in relation to comorbidity, Saitz (2007) emphasizes the need for good case management where all the clinical needs of the patient are addressed in a coordinated fashion. Although there is limited research on treating comorbidities, reviewers tend to agree that treatments that work for a single disorder will lead to some improvements in dually diagnosed patients, if not in both disorders (Mills et al., 2009).

Addressing stigma

Few individuals with alcohol use disorders seek treatment for their disorder. The poor treatment of alcohol use disorders contrasts with much better rates for treatment of depression in Australia (Slade et al., 2009). The highly successful campaigns internationally addressing the stigma, public literacy, and treatment response to depression may be highly instructive in improving treatment of alcohol use disorders (Teesson et al., 2010).

There have been three core components of campaigns to improve the community's response to depression: the availability of effective interventions, better coordination of care services, and public campaigns to destigmatize depression and educate the public and professionals about its recognition and treatment (Teesson et al., 2010). There is evidence that the effectiveness of treatment for alcohol use disorders (Morley et al., 2006) is comparable with that of treatments for other mental and physical disorders (McLellan et al., 1997). Despite this very few seek treatment. Alcohol use disorders remain highly stigmatized (Room, 2005) with affected individuals expressing a lack of confidence in treatment options (Proudfoot & Teesson, 2001). In addition, the treatment response to alcohol use disorders is underfunded and poorly coordinated. Since stigma and poor service coordination play a significant role in the low treatment rates, the successful depression campaigns may provide guidance on how to improve treatment for alcohol use disorders (Teesson et al., 2010).

Alcohol and pregnancy

Drinking more than seven standard drinks per week during pregnancy can increase the risks of developmental and cognitive disabilities in the child. Despite this, more than 20% of women worldwide consume alcohol during pregnancy (Stade, Bailey, Dzendoletas, Sgro, Dowswell, & Bennett, 2009). The recent Cochrane Review by Stade and colleagues (2009) found that although there is a paucity of good research, there is some evidence that psychological and educational interventions, such as the brief motivational interventions discussed above, can increase abstinence among pregnant women and women planning to become pregnant. Apart from the obvious benefit to parents, there would be a significant cost–benefit to society in providing such interventions to offset the life-long costs of birth defects that can be caused by alcohol use during pregnancy.

Summary

Assessment is an important first step in the treatment of alcohol problems. There are a range of standardized measures of alcohol dependence and screening instruments, such as AUDIT and AUDIT-C, which can be used to determine the severity of a client's alcohol-related problems. Given the high prevalence of depression and anxiety among heavy drinkers, assessment of comorbid psychiatric disorders is also recommended.

One-to-one intensive interventions are not required for everyone who has a problem with alcohol use. Public health interventions to advise drinkers of safe levels of drinking have a role to play. So too does screening and brief intervention for hazardous alcohol use in primary health care and other settings, where adults who drink hazardously and harmfully are to be found. Hazardous drinkers can be given simple advice on how to reduce or moderate their alcohol consumption. Moderation rather than abstinence is an appropriate therapeutic goal for patients with mild to moderate levels of alcohol dependence. Patients with more severe forms of dependence should be encouraged to become abstinent.

There are several treatment approaches available for patients whose alcohol problems have resisted self-help efforts to moderate or quit. One of the oldest is the self-help fellowship of AA, which is of assistance in helping some alcohol-dependent people to remain abstinent but it is not attractive to all patients.

Psychological interventions that are of value in the treatment of alcohol dependence include CBT, MET, TSF, and FMT. These treatments seem to be of equivalent efficacy in unselected patients and there does not appear to be any particular value in attempting to match patients to treatment on any basis other than patient choice. The briefer versions of CBT and MET recommend themselves because they minimize time and costs.

Pharmacotherapies such as disulfiram, naltrexone, and acomprosate may assist some patients to remain abstinent by reducing relapse to drinking. Ensuring adequate compliance with the drugs is a major issue. Newer drugs that are being trialled with promising results include the anticonvulsant topiramate and the anaesthetic sedative GHB.

Cost–benefit analyses support a stepped care approach, starting with minimal intervention and proceeding to more intensive psychosocial and pharmacological interventions as needed. Web-based, mail, and telephone interventions can be used as a first step in a stepped care approach. They also reduce costs and reach different sub-populations to standard face-to-face interventions.

Treatments for alcohol use disorders are of significant value to society. Miller, Walters, and Bennett (2001) estimated that, in the USA, typically one-third of those undergoing any treatment for alcohol dependence will be abstinent at 1-year follow-up. Approximately another third are improved, leaving one-third unimproved. The UKATT Research Team (2005) found that the treatments they used saved about five times the health, social, and criminal justice costs of leaving alcohol problems untreated. In his review of treatments for all drugs and alcohol, Saitz (2007, p. 60) pointed out that the benefits to society from treating drug and alcohol disorders outweigh their costs "4–12-fold (depending on drug and treatment type)".

Nicotine 6

Introduction

Along with alcohol and caffeine, tobacco is one of the most widely used psychoactive substances in the general population. When smoked it has a higher dependence liability than the opiates, alcohol, and other controlled substances (Anthony, Warner, & Kessler, 1994).

Over the past century evidence has accumulated about the serious adverse effects of tobacco smoking on the health of smokers as well as the adverse effects of involuntary exposure to tobacco on non-smokers. The list of diseases caused by exposure to tobacco smoke is ever increasing (US Department of Health and Human Services, 2004, 2006). According to the latest Global Burden of Disease Report, diseases caused by smoking tobacco include: "lung cancer, upper aerodigestive cancer, stomach cancer, liver cancer, pancreas cancer, cervix uteri cancer, bladder cancer, leukemia, COPD [chronic obstructive pulmonary disease], other respiratory diseases, IHD [ischaemic heart disease], stroke, selected other cardiovascular diseases except hypertensive heart disease, and selected other medical causes in adults over 30 years of age; fire injuries, maternal outcomes, and perinatal conditions" (Lopez, Mathers, Ezzati, Jamison, & Murray, 2006, p. 243).

Smoking is second only to high blood pressure as a risk factor for death worldwide. The Global Burden of Disease study estimates that tobacco smoking is the fourth highest cause of disease burden in the world, after low birth weight, high blood pressure and unsafe sex (Lopez et al., 2006). This same report calculates that approximately 4.8 million deaths per annum can be attributed to smoking, with the rate among males three times that among females.

Research in the USA and elsewhere has found that around 70% of smokers want to quit and that opportunistic interventions from health professionals such as GPs, dentists, pharmacists, and others can motivate smokers to quit (Fiore et al., 2008). Given the burden of disease caused by smoking, and the low cost of smoking cessation treatments, these brief opportunistic interventions are among the most cost-effective in medicine (Lopez et al., 2006).

Assessment

Assessment should include three aspects: motivation to quit, nicotine dependence, and smoking history (including past quit attempts). Motivation to quit is important initially, as it relates directly to how likely an individual is to take the first step of ceasing to smoke. Assessment of motivation to quit smoking may be done simply by direct questioning: "Do you want to stop smoking for good?"; "Are you interested in making a serious attempt to stop in the near future?"; and "Are you interested in receiving help with your quit attempt?" (West, 2004). An uncertain or ambivalent response to these questions may indicate a need for motivational interviewing techniques (Rubak, Sandbaek, Lauritzen, & Christensen, 2005).

Level of dependence is an indicator of the likelihood that a person will remain abstinent if they quit. Research suggests that persons who are more severely dependent on nicotine may have greater difficulty in remaining abstinent, and so may require a more intensive intervention (e.g., the use of nicotine replacement therapy, atypical antidepressants or partial nicotine agonists). Brief qualitative questions can be used to assess level of dependence. West (2004) suggests two questions: "Do you find it difficult not to smoke in situations where you would normally smoke?" and "Have you tried to stop smoking for good in the past but found that you could not?"

Perhaps the most widely used quantitative measure of nicotine dependence in clinical settings is the Fagerström Test for Nicotine Dependence (see Table 6.1; Heatherton, Kozlowski, Frecker, & Fagerström, 1991; West, 2004). This is a measure of nicotine dependence with a score ranging from 0 to 10, with higher scores indicating higher levels of dependence.

Questions about the smoking history of clients may also be useful. This could include the number of years they have regularly smoked, and history of previous quit attempts (how many and what

TABLE 6.1

The Fagerström Test for Nicotine Dependence (Heatherton et al., 1991, p. 1125)

a How soon after waking do you smoke your first cigarette?
  3 Within 5 minutes
  2 6–30 minutes
  1 31–60 minutes

b Do you find it difficult to abstain from smoking in places where it is forbidden?
  1 Yes
  0 No

c Which cigarette would you hate to give up?
  1 The first one in the morning
  0 Any other

d How many cigarettes a day do you smoke?
  0 10 or less
  1 11 to 20
  2 21 to 30
  3 31 or more

e Do you smoke more frequently in the morning than in the rest of the day?
  1 Yes
  0 No

f Do you smoke even though you are sick in bed for most of the day?
  1 Yes
  0 No

Score: 0–2 = very low dependence; 3–4 = low dependence; 5 = medium dependence; 6–7 = high dependence; 8+ = very high dependence.

© Karl Fagerström, reproduced with permission.

interventions, if any, were used to assist them). This knowledge can help to formulate an appropriate intervention plan. Persons who have smoked for many years, from a young age, and who have previously attempted to quit smoking, may require more intensive assistance to stop smoking.

Monitoring of withdrawal symptoms is an important component of the smoking cessation intervention (Fiore et al., 2008). As withdrawal symptoms are predictive of relapse to smoking, careful attention to this possibility needs to be part of planning the quit attempt. Symptoms of nicotine withdrawal include craving for a cigarette, depressed mood, difficulty falling asleep, awakening at night, irritability, frustration or anger, anxiety, difficulty concentrating, restlessness, and increased appetite. West and Ussher (2010, p. 429) found that the single question: "How much have you craved cigarettes today?" was reliable, and as sensitive as longer measures. Severity is rated on a 6-point scale – 0 = not at all, 1 = hardly at all, 2 = a little, 3 = somewhat, 4 = quite a bit, 5 = a great deal.

Assessment should also consider comorbid conditions including depression and anxiety disorders. Depression makes it less likely that attempts to quit smoking will be successful (Anda, Williamson, Escobedo, Mast, Giovino, & Remington, 1990). Depressed mood is also a common symptom of nicotine withdrawal (Madden et al., 1997). Researchers suggest extended patient care is needed for those with pre-existing depression (Covey, 1999; Fiore et al., 2008). There is also an association between anxiety disorders and smoking and smoking cessation. It has been shown that, similarly to depression, persons with anxiety also find it more difficult to stop smoking and may require more intensive or extended clinical intervention (Zvolensky, Bernstein, Marshall, & Feldner, 2006).

Interventions

A variety of approaches to smoking cessation have been developed. The most comprehensive guidelines are maintained through the US Department of Health and Human Services: Clinical Practice Guidelines (Fiore et al., 2008). A brief summary of these guidelines highlighting practical clinical applications is also published (Hays, Ebbert, & Sood, 2009). Box 6.1 lists the 5A's model for clinician use provided by the guidelines (Fiore et al., 2008, p. 39).

Once a person is willing to make a quit attempt, then assistance can be given in the formulation of a quit plan (Fiore et al., 2008). This may consist of the following elements.

1 Setting a date for quitting tobacco use. This date should ideally be within 1 or 2 weeks.
2 Assisting the client with his or her preparation for the quit attempt. This may include a number of elements, including:
   (a) the client telling others that a quitting attempt is being made and asking for their support;
   (b) removing cigarettes from the client's environment;

(c) going over previous attempts to quit (if any) and examining what elements were helpful or not so helpful to the client; and

(d) examining anything that may be a challenge to the success of the quit attempt, particularly in the early stages, e.g., withdrawal symptoms.

Among the more important issues to consider are the following.

1 Make abstinence the goal of the quit attempt, as research suggests that any smoking increases the chances that a full relapse to smoking will occur (Mattick & Baillie, 1992).

2 Inform the patient about the nature of withdrawal symptoms and the length of time for which they are likely to continue. Withdrawal symptoms typically begin a few hours after cessation of smoking, and peak at 24 to 72 hours (Mattick & Baillie, 1992). They may continue in a less intense fashion for between a week and a month.

3 Be aware of the triggers for relapse. These include drinking alcohol, and sharing a household with smokers. The client might consider avoiding drinking alcohol for a short period; and perhaps coordinate the quit attempt with other smokers, or make plans to maintain abstinence in the household.

Interventions for smoking can be broadly classified into psychosocial, pharmacological, and "other". In general, research has found that both psychological and pharmacological intervention are effective. One major meta-analysis found that adding pharmacotherapies (e.g., nicotine replacement therapy [NRT], bupropion) to nonpharmacological methods increased the probability of cessation, as well as abstinence rates at 12 months, by 1.5 to 3 times. The number needed to treat to have one patient stop smoking ranged from 8 to 21 (Bala, Lesniak, & Strzeszynski, 2008a).

Psychosocial interventions

Counselling and advice

Given the difficulties associated with achieving and maintaining abstinence from smoking, there are a number of ways in which an individual may be informed of the pitfalls to success and suggestions made to reduce the chances that they will return to smoking (Fiore et al., 2008). This may involve a brief intervention in which the client is informed of some of the issues to consider regarding the quit attempt, and some of the things that can be done to make success more likely. In fact, research on psychosocial treatments such as physician's advice and individual and group counselling has shown that they increase the probability of smoking abstinence and these effects last at least 12 months (Bala & Lesniak, 2007).

A recent meta-analysis has found that even brief simple advice from a doctor increases the likelihood of quitting smoking, and remaining a non-smoker 12 months later (Stead, Bergson, & Lancaster, 2008a). There is some evidence that more advice has better outcomes, as does follow-up support. An important issue brought out in one major review was the impact of the attitude of the physician to efforts of their patients to quit smoking. This research found that the pessimism of some GPs about the effectiveness of treatment prevented them from broaching the subject with their patients (Vogt, Hall, & Marteau, 2007), thereby missing an important opportunity to intervene to improve their patients' health.

Another meta-analysis found that individual counselling could help smokers quit, but there was not enough evidence to decide whether more intensive counselling was better (Lancaster & Stead, 2005a). Individual counselling was defined as one or more sessions between a client and a trained smoking-cessation counsellor (counselling by doctors or nurses as part of clinical care was excluded). Sessions all involved more than 10 minutes of contact, with most also including further telephone contact for support.

A further meta-analysis of group counselling for smoking cessation found that group programmes were more effective than no intervention or minimal contact interventions (Stead & Lancaster, 2005). The authors concluded that "Group programmes are more effective for helping people to stop smoking than being given self-help materials without face-to-face instruction and group support. The chances of quitting are approximately doubled. It is unclear whether groups are better than individual counselling or other advice, but they are more effective than no treatment. Not all smokers making a quit attempt want to attend group meetings, but for those who do, they are likely to be helpful" (Stead & Lancaster, 2005, p. 2).

Self-help and telephone counselling for smoking

A meta-analysis of the use of self-help materials for smoking cessation found a small benefit on quit rates compared with no intervention (Lancaster & Stead, 2005b). However, if other effective interventions are also being used, such as advice from a health professional or nicotine replacement therapy, addition of the self-help material showed no increased benefit. There was some evidence that tailoring self-help material to the individual may improve smoking outcomes. Thus, self-help materials may be best reserved for those who do not want face-to-face counselling or advice, but are willing to attempt to quit smoking.

Telephone counselling may also be preferred by people who do not want face-to-face counselling. A meta-analytic review has found that telephone counselling, either alone or in conjunction with other interventions, is effective in promoting smoking cessation, and multiple sessions are likely to be more helpful (Stead, Perera, & Lancaster, 2006).

Pharmacological interventions

Nicotine replacement therapy

The development of nicotine replacement therapy (NRT) has been a major advance in smoking cessation. Smokers who have a medium to high score on the Fagerström Test for Nicotine Dependence (see Table 6.1; Heatherton et al., 1991) are likely to be addicted to nicotine. Such smokers may experience withdrawal symptoms during the first 2 weeks of not smoking. NRT is designed to reduce craving for a cigarette and helps to prevent these withdrawal symptoms (Pomerleau & Pomerleau, 1988). It is available as transdermal skin patches that deliver the nicotine slowly and as gum, nasal sprays, inhalers, and sublingual tablets/lozenges that deliver the nicotine to the brain more quickly than from skin patches, but slower than from smoking cigarettes (Stead, Perera, Bullen, Mant, & Lancaster, 2008b).

Stead and colleagues (Stead, Perera, Bullen, Mant, & Lancaster, 2008b) carried out a meta-analysis that included 132 trials with 40,000 people in the main analysis. They found that all forms of NRT were effective in assisting smoking cessation, and that they increased the rate of quitting by 50–70%, regardless of setting. They found no difference in effectiveness between the various forms of NRT. While more intensive levels of psychosocial support benefited the process of quitting, NRT can be successful without such support. Heavier smokers may need higher doses of NRT, but limited evidence suggests that patches show no further benefit beyond 8 weeks. Combining the patch with another faster acting form can increase the likelihood of success. Also some studies in the meta-analysis suggest that starting NRT before actually quitting may prove an additional benefit.

Some adverse effects were found depending on the type of NRT used. The patches can irritate the skin and the gum and tablets can irritate the inside of the mouth. There is no evidence to date that NRT increases the risk of heart attack.

Antidepressant drugs

Antidepressant drugs may be particularly effective in assisting people to stop smoking. A broad range of antidepressant drugs has been trialled as aids to nicotine withdrawal, and are of particular relevance for those with a history of prior episodes of depression, or for those who have a history of failed quit attempts who may require a more intensive intervention to help them to quit successfully.

A recent meta-analysis has concluded that the antidepressants nortriptyline and bupropion (Zyban) are both effective in aiding long-term smoking cessation (Hughes, Stead, & Lancaster, 2007). Bupropion has effects on dopaminergic and noradrenergic transmission, and nortriptyline is a tricyclic antidepressant with adrenergic activity. These two antidepressant drugs were found in an earlier review to pose little or no risk of dependence (Hughes, Stead, & Lancaster, 2000). As with most drugs, they produce some adverse reactions, but they are rarely serious or cause the individual to stop taking the medication (Hughes et al., 2007). Other antidepressants such as selective serotonin reuptake inhibitors, specifically fluoxetine, paroxetine, or sertraline, and the monoamine oxidase inhibitors moclobemide or selegiline, showed no significant effects.

The meta-analysis found no superiority in efficacy of nortriptyline or bupropion over the other, and similar efficacy to NRT. Studies comparing the efficacy of bupropion with the nicotine receptor partial agonist varenicline (see below), however, showed lower quit rates with bupropion (Hughes et al., 2007).

Nicotine receptor partial agonists

This group of drugs, which includes varenicline and cytosine, has shown particular potential in aiding smoking cessation. In one large meta-analysis varenicline was found to increase the chances of long-term smoking cessation between two to three times that of no added pharmacotherapy (Cahill, Stead Lindsay, & Lancaster, 2008b). It was found to be superior to bupropion and showed a modest benefit over NRT. A further large review found varenicline to be more cost-effective than antidepressant pharmacotherapies (Hoogen-doorn, Welsing, & Rutten-van Molken, 2008). Varenicline can cause mild to moderate nausea in patients but this subsides over time. Further research is needed to clarify whether it causes adverse events such as depression, agitation, and suicidal thoughts (Cahill et al., 2008b). There has not been sufficient research on cytosine, but it is another intervention deserving further research.

Clonidine: an antihypertensive drug

A meta-analytic review suggests that clonidine may be helpful in reducing drug and alcohol withdrawal symptoms and thereby increase the likelihood of quitting smoking. But the quality of research on clonidine is not high and researchers suggest it could be used as a last-line treatment for people who do not respond to anti-depressants and NRT (Gourlay, Stead, & Benowitz, 2004).

Nicobrevin

Nicobrevin contains quinine, menthyl valerate, camphor and eucalyptus oil. A review found that there has been no efficacy research carried out on this product (Stead & Lancaster, 2006). Until such research is done, it cannot be recommended for use.

Nicotine vaccine

Nicotine vaccines produce antibodies that bind nicotine and prevent it from entering the brain (Murtagh & Foerster, 2007). They have been proposed as a possible means of preventing uptake of smoking, assisting withdrawal from smoking, and preventing relapse to smoking. Reviews of the research using animal models as well as early human trials suggest they have potential as a therapy for nicotine dependence (Hall, 2002; Maurer & Bachmann, 2007).

Other therapies and interventions

Recent critical reviews have analysed the effectiveness of various other interventions to reduce smoking. From these it was concluded that both *aversive smoking* (Hajek & Stead, 2001) and *acupuncture* (White, Rampes, Liu, Stead, & Campbell, 2011) had little empirical support but that further research may be justified. Research on providing *feedback on bio-markers* (e.g., biological indices of smoking-related harm, harm exposure, or genetic susceptibility to disease) has also had some promising outcomes, but more research is required to determine its effectiveness (McClure, 2001).

Randomized controlled trials on *hypnotherapy* for smoking cessation have found no support for this therapy (Abbot, Stead, White, Barnes, & Ernst, 2000). The same is true for the use of *biomedical risk assessments* (e.g., exhaled carbon monoxide [CO], or genetic susceptibility to lung cancer) (Bize, Burnand, Mueller, & Cornuz, 2007).

Competitions and rewards work to help people quit, but make no difference to long-term cessation rates (Cahill & Perera, 2008). Bala, Strzeszynski, and Cahill (2008) analysed the evidence regarding the effectiveness of *mass media campaigns* and found that they can be effective in reducing smoking in adults. However, the research has been of variable quality and actual effects hard to quantify. Another review looked at the efficacy of *financial compensation* for quitting through healthcare services, and found that this could increase quit rates at a low cost per quitter. Studies to date have not been of a very high methodological quality (Reda, Kaper, Fikretler, Severens, & van Schayck, 2009).

In order to assist with depression and weight gain associated with quitting, *exercise* is often recommended as an aid to smoking cessation. A systematic review found that although exercise has some positive effects, there is insufficient research of a good quality to draw conclusions about its efficacy (Ussher, Taylor, & Faulkner, 2008). Another review looking at *weight control* interventions as an aid to smoking cessation concluded that although exercise had no impact on weight gain at the end of treatment, it may have reduced weight in the longer term after quitting (Parsons, Shraim, Inglis, Aveyard, & Hajek, 2009). General advice about weight control during treatment does not reduce weight gain and may in fact contribute to the failure of a quit attempt. Individualized interventions, very low calorie diets, and CBT were more likely to reduce weight gain without reducing abstinence. Parsons and colleagues (2009, p. 2) found that "bupropion, fluoxetine, nicotine replacement therapy, and probably varenicline all reduced weight gain while being used", but these effects tended not to be maintained 1 year later.

Populations with smoking-related illnesses

Several large systematic reviews have been completed on smoking cessation programmes for ill and hospitalized patients. In the case of people with chronic obstructive pulmonary disease (COPD), Wagena, van der Meer, Ostelo, Jacobs, and van Schayck (2004, p. 806) concluded that "the most effective intervention for prolonged smoking cessation in patients with COPD is the combination of nicotine replacement therapy, coupled with an intensive, prolonged relapse prevention programme". Barth, Critchley, and Bengel (2008) reviewed interventions in coronary patients and found that psychosocial interventions were effective but further research was needed on a broader range of therapies, including pharmacological therapies and combinations of these with psychosocial interventions. Rigotti, Munafo, and Stead Lindsay (2007) found that quit smoking programmes that began while people were in hospital, and included follow-up support for at least 1 month after discharge, were effective. This applied regardless of diagnosis on entering hospital.

Interventions in the workplace

A review of interventions for smoking cessation conducted in the workplace found that individual and group counselling and pharmacological treatments were equally effective when administered in the workplace as elsewhere (Cahill, Moher, & Lancaster, 2008a). The review also found that "social and environmental support, competitions and incentives, and comprehensive programmes do not show a clear benefit in helping smokers to quit at work" (p. 2).

A note on smoking reduction

Stead and Lancaster (2007) reviewed the literature on interventions for smoking reduction, and found that although some treatments such as NRT reduce smoking, the benefits to health of cutting down rather than quitting have not been demonstrated. They contend that the notion of "cutting down" can undermine that of quitting, which has clear-cut health benefits, and the use of NRT in this context should be considered a precursor to quitting rather than as a way to reduce the health risks of smoking.

Tobacco harm reduction

Snus is a Swedish smokeless tobacco product that is low in carcino-genic nitrosamines. It is a moist form of snuff, which is typically placed under the upper lip. Used in this way it does not tend to induce spitting that occurs with other chewing tobacco products. It is proposed as a potential substitute to smoking tobacco to reduce the harm caused by smoking. The increased use of snus in Sweden has reduced the prevalence of smoking and smoking-related disease (Hall & Gartner, 2009). Snus is currently banned in most of Europe and Australia and, while it is legally available in the USA, its use is strongly discouraged there (Gartner, Hall, Vos, Bertram, Wallace, & Lim, 2007).

There is considerable controversy around the use of snus (Gartner et al., 2007), with opponents arguing, among other things, that intro-ducing these products will increase tobacco use without significantly reducing smoking. Because using smokeless tobacco is not harmless, this may lead to an increase in harms associated with tobacco use.

Gartner and colleagues (2007) modelled the potential individual and population health effects of snus. They concluded that there is little difference in life expectancies of individual smokers who switch to snus compared with those who stop smoking altogether. They also found a net benefit to the population if sufficient inveterate smokers converted to snus. Proponents of snus argue that with the support of appropriate legislation, legalization of snus could lead to significant improvements in public health (Hall & Gartner, 2009).

Summary

Tobacco smoking results in a huge burden of disease and because of this interventions to assist smokers to stop are among the most cost-effective in medicine. It is important that health professionals are willing to broach the subject of the patient's smoking as a part of good preventive health care.

Once it is established that a person is a smoker, they should be advised about the effects of smoking, and assessed for their willing-ness to quit and level of dependence. The major question of the smoker's nicotine dependence can be assessed by brief questions or the Fagerström scale. Its relevance is in deciding whether the smoker may be helped to deal with withdrawal symptoms by use of more intensive interventions.

Once the decision has been made to quit, the smoker should be encouraged to make a quit plan assisted through motivational strategies. Support should continue for some time after quitting to help prevent relapse to smoking, and if relapse occurs, the smoker should be encouraged to make further attempts to quit in the future.

Interventions can be effective, whether given in the community, the doctor's surgery, pharmacies or the workplace. Effective interventions include:

- brief doctor's advice to give up smoking;
- individual or group counselling;
- self-help and telephone counselling;
- nicotine replacement therapy (all types);
- antidepressant medications bupropion and nortriptyline;
- nicotine receptor partial agonist varenicline.

Cannabis 7

Introduction

Cannabis is the most commonly used illicit drug in the world, although its use may be declining among younger adults in developed countries (United Nations Office on Drugs and Crime (UNODC), 2009). Cannabis comes from the *cannabis sativa* plant. Its primary psychoactive ingredient is THC, which is a central nervous system depressant that has hallucinogenic properties. Cannabis may be used as marijuana, hashish, and hashish oil. Marijuana is the least potent version and consists of the dried leaves and flowers of the plant. Hashish is the dried resin from the cannabis plant and a stronger version of cannabis, while hashish oil is the most potent derivative. A number of terms are applied to cannabis products, including marijuana, dope, mull, pot, weed, skunk, and grass. Forms of cannabis grown hydroponically (i.e., in an enriched substrate without soil) are often known as "hydro".

Marijuana and hashish can be smoked, with or without tobacco in a joint, in a pipe or a water pipe (called a 'bong'). While bongs maximize the amount of THC consumed, they also increase the amount of tar and other harmful materials consumed per dose, compared with joints (Gowing, Ali, & White, 2000). Hashish oil can be absorbed by cigarette papers and smoked with tobacco.

The effects of smoking cannabis are almost immediate, as the active ingredient is absorbed directly from the lungs into the blood stream. All types of cannabis can be cooked into food and eaten or drunk, but this takes longer to produce effects, which makes it a less popular method with users. Digesting cannabis does not carry the respiratory and other physical risks that are associated with smoking, but its effects can be unpredictable as it is difficult to judge how much to take at any one time, due to the time elapsing between eating and experiencing its effects.

Recently THC has been trialled for medical uses such as to relieve the nausea associated with cancer chemotherapy; for people with spinal cord injuries; and for people with damage to their gut lining (Pacher, Batkai, & Kunos, 2006). However, its use is controversial because of the harms associated with smoking and the fact that this use is not approved. Using a vaporizer (oral spray) to inhale the cannabis may be a suitable substitute for smoking for these medical purposes. Medical cannabis use is legal in some countries.

Cannabis was initially thought by many to be a "soft" drug, but with increased use of the drug worldwide and greater research on its effects, this can no longer be considered the case. Like most other psychoactive substances that produce euphoric effects, the regular, heavy use of cannabis may result in a cannabis-dependence syndrome (Swift, Copeland, & Hall, 1997). Apart from causing dependence, chronic heavy use of cannabis probably increases the risk of some cancers, chronic bronchitis, permanent damage to the airways, and increases the risk of heart disease. It also increases the risks of traffic and other accidents if users drive while intoxicated.

Chronic use can also adversely affect the mental health of users by increasing the risk of depression, anxiety (including panic attacks), and memory problems, as well as psychosis in vulnerable individuals (Hall, 2009). As with tobacco smoking, babies whose mothers smoked cannabis during pregnancy are more likely to be born prematurely with a lower birth weight. In Australia, it is estimated that cannabis use causes around 16% of all illicit drug-related hospital costs – second only to opioids (Collins & Lapsley, 2008b).

Prevention

Significant numbers of young people use cannabis on a regular basis, and age of initiation for most people is the teenage years. Recent research suggests that early cannabis use may lead to later drug problems (Degenhardt, Coffey, Carlin, Swift, Moore, & Patton, 2010b). Thus research on prevention has focused largely on school students. A recent large-scale review by Faggiano and colleagues (Faggiano, Vigna-Taglianti, Versino, Zambon, Borraccino, & Lemma, 2008) classified research findings for drug prevention programmes under three headings:

1 skills-focused: teaching peer-based refusal/resistance and social/ life skills;
2 affective-focused: addressing psychological factors such as self-esteem and self-awareness; and
3 knowledge-focused; teaching about the negative outcomes from drug use.

Other types of prevention programmes have been used, but they have either not been evaluated or the research is not of a high standard.

Faggiano et al. (2008) found that compared with usual school curricula, skills-focused programmes had positive effects on mediating variables such as drug knowledge, decision making, self-esteem and peer pressure resistance, as well as on drug-taking behaviours. Although affective-focused and knowledge-focused programmes were found to improve some mediating skills (such as drug knowledge), there was no evidence that they prevented drug use.

Assessment

Assessment may comprise a structured clinical interview, in which key data pertaining to demographics, drug use, family history, pattern and history of cannabis use, past treatment experiences, and criminal history are obtained. In addition, clients may complete a number of self-administered instruments.

It can be useful to obtain a measure of the client's self-efficacy, or situational confidence to resist cannabis use in a range of situations. One such measure is the Situational Confidence Questionnaire (SCQ-39, Annis & Graham, 1988), although it is not cannabis-specific. Such a measure can be used to monitor clinically relevant changes over time, as well as provide important information about the client's profile of cannabis use at the time of assessment. Another questionnaire that may be useful to help monitor symptoms throughout treatment is the Cannabis Problems Questionnaire (CPQ, Copeland et al., 2005) and the adolescent version (CPQ-A-S, Martin, Proudfoot, Vogl, Swift, & Copeland, 2010). A more general measure of drug abuse that has been found to be a useful assessment of clients with cannabis problems in research or the clinic is the Drug Abuse Screening Test (DAST, Yudko, Lozhkina, & Fouts, 2007).

For diagnosis of cannabis dependence, questions assessing the DSM criteria should be used to obtain a thorough appraisal of the client's cannabis dependence symptoms. In addition, the Severity of Dependence Scale (SDS, Gossop et al., 1995) has been adapted from its primary purpose of assessment of heroin dependence to cannabis dependence (Swift et al., 1997). This scale provides an assessment of psychological aspects of cannabis dependence. Of these measures of dependence, the SDS is the briefest and most clinically useful instrument (Swift, Copeland, & Hall, 1998).

Comorbid drug and mental disorders are common among cannabis-dependent persons seeking treatment. They can influence the course and severity of the disorder and the treatment process. Thus the assessment should also probe for the coexistence of other drug and alcohol disorders and other psychiatric disorders. Brief screeners can be useful in this context, e.g., the Depression Anxiety Stress Scale (DASS, Lovibond & Lovibond, 1995); Kessler's 10 Psychological Distress Scale (K10, Kessler, 1996); Alcohol Use Disorders Identification Test (AUDIT, Saunders et al., 1993); a psychosis screener (Degenhardt et al., 2005). A good source of information on such screeners is the review by Dawe et al. (2002).

Interventions

Over the past decade, treatment-seeking for cannabis disorders has increased dramatically in many developed countries. As with other drugs of abuse, heavy cannabis users who cease taking the drug can exhibit symptoms of withdrawal (Budney & Hughes, 2006), which can make it difficult to cut down or abstain from using the drug (e.g., Copersino et al., 2006; Cornelius, Chung, Martin, Wood, & Clark, 2008). People who seek treatment for their cannabis dependence are more likely to have other drug and alcohol problems as well as comorbid psychiatric disorders such as depression and personality disorders (Agosti & Levin, 2004; Arendt, Rosenberg, Foldager, Perto, & Munk-Jorgensen, 2007).

In response to the increased demand for treatment, various psychological and pharmacological interventions for cannabis withdrawal and dependence have been assessed in recent years, but the field is still in its infancy.

Psychological interventions (see Appendix on pp. 93–98)

Psychosocial interventions that have been trialled for treatment of cannabis dependence include single and group CBT and MET, contingency management, social support, drug counselling, case management, the community reinforcement approach, family therapy, and family support therapy. Two recent large-scale reviews have concluded that such psychotherapies assist in treating cannabis disorders and combinations of two or more therapy types have shown particular promise (Benyamina, Lecacheux, Blecha, Reynaud, & Lukasiewcz, 2008; Nordstrom & Levin, 2007). There is very little evidence that any one psychological intervention or combination of interventions is more effective than any other. There is a need for more large-scale randomized trials comparing these treatments. Adding vouchers to counselling treatment, for maintaining abstinence, has only been shown to be effective while the vouchers are offered (i.e., during treatment). Vouchers appear to improve motivation during treatment, and when combined with CBT or MET to improve longer-term coping skills, enabling significant improvements to be maintained post-treatment. As yet there is no clear evidence that longer-term therapies are more effective than those of shorter duration.

Reviewers for the Cochrane Collaboration (Denis, Lavie, Fatseas, & Auriacombe, 2006) concluded that counselling approaches may have a beneficial effect on treatment outcome, but the outcome of treatment is often to reduce cannabis use and dependence symptoms and problems rather than to achieve abstinence. Overall, abstinence rates were low post-treatment, indicating that it is difficult to treat cannabis dependence in outpatient settings when abstinence is the desired goal.

Although cannabis-dependent clients show the same problems and symptoms as cocaine-dependent clients, these symptoms are less severe than in cocaine-dependent clients (Hathaway, Callaghan, Macdonald, & Erickson, 2009). Thus, a strict abstinence-based agenda may be less suitable in treating cannabis dependence than adopting the aim of controlled use, which the research above suggests may be more achievable in the short term. However, in the case of clients with comorbid severe mental disorders, abstinence from all drugs and alcohol may be essential for maintaining mental health (Cleary, Hunt, Matheson, Siegfried, & Walter, 2008).

Pharmacological interventions

Several pharmacotherapies have been evaluated for withdrawal and relapse prevention in cannabis use disorders. Much of this research has been laboratory based using small samples (Benyamina et al.,

2008; Nordstrom & Levin, 2007). Bupropion, nefazodone (both anti-depressants), naltrexone (an opiate receptor blocking agent) and divalproex (an anticonvulsant) showed no impact on withdrawal symptoms and had adverse side effects. Mirtazapine (another anti-depressant) in combination with CBT was found, in a larger study, to improve mood with few adverse side effects, but it had no effect on withdrawal symptoms. Oral THC has shown most promise in managing withdrawal symptoms. Further large-scale studies are required to assess the value of mirtazapine and oral THC in managing cannabis withdrawal and dependence.

Pharmacotherapies that have been assessed for relapse prevention in cannabis use disorders (i.e., to maintain abstinence) include rimonabant (a cannaboid receptor blocking agent), oral THC, divalproex, buspirone (an anxiolytic drug) and atomoxetine (a drug used to treat adult attention-deficit hyperactivity disorder). Of these, rimonabant and perhaps buspirone and oral THC have shown the most promise (Benyamina et al., 2008). These studies have used very small samples so larger-scale trials are necessary before it is clear whether they improve longer-term outcomes for cannabis dependence.

Treating comorbidity

Where an individual has a severe mental disorder such as schizo-phrenia or bipolar disorder, continued use of drugs and alcohol can significantly exacerbate the mental illness, increasing psychotic symptoms and acute hospitalization. Thus it is most important that such drug use is identified and treated as soon as possible. Treatments that have been trialled for this group include long-term integrated care, non-integrated intensive case management, CBT, MET, CBT with MET, and skills training. This research has not yet established whether any of these psychosocial treatments are effective in this group with comorbid severe mental disorders (Cleary et al., 2008).

For some psychiatric conditions, research has suggested that the pharmacotherapy that is used to treat the (non-drug) psychiatric condition can have a positive impact on comorbid drug use as well. For example, the use of lithium in adolescent patients with bipolar disorder has also been found to reduce cannabis use (Geller et al., 1998). Similarly fluoxetine (Cornelius et al., 1999) significantly reduced cannabis use in an inpatient group of depressed alcoholics who also met criteria for cannabis dependence. Again these studies have been small and larger replications are needed before any confident conclusions can be drawn about the efficacy of pharmacotherapy for cannabis use in individuals with comorbid psychiatric conditions.

Summary

Evidence has emerged in the past few decades that some individuals can become dependent on cannabis and regular cannabis smoking can be associated with significant harms.

The number of persons seeking assistance to stop or reduce their cannabis use has increased as the prevalence of cannabis use has increased in the population. Psychosocial interventions such as CBT and MET can be effective in treating cannabis dependence, although as with other drugs of dependence, several attempts may be necessary to attain either controlled use or abstinence. Unfortunately these treatments have not been shown to assist in reducing cannabis use in individuals with comorbid severe mental disorders. At this stage, no pharmacotherapies can be recommended for treating cannabis disorders.

The harms of smoking cannabis are now clear and modestly effective treatments for cannabis disorders are available. It is likely that the earlier intervention is begun, the less costly and more effective it will be (Copeland & Maxwell, 2007). So it is important to ensure that these facts are more widely disseminated in the community and that GPs are adequately resourced to either provide brief interventions or advice, or to refer patients to treatment at the earliest opportunity.

Appendix to Chapter 7: A CBT intervention and relapse prevention for cannabis dependence

The basic structure of an intervention using CBT for cannabis is described below. The intervention outlined is based on an outpatient treatment delivered to an individual client that is designed to occupy 6 structured therapy sessions of approximately 1 hour.

At a single assessment session, undertaken in the week prior to the commencement of therapy, key data are obtained from the client and an outline of the nature and content of the therapy is given. Ideally, the timing and physical location of the therapy sessions should be as consistent as possible; that is, appointments for the same time and day should be made for each subsequent week, and the place should be held constant. This may help to optimize the establishment of a working rapport with the therapist and help the client to become comfortable with the therapeutic arrangements.

Session 1

The main elements of this session involve setting the scene and introducing motivational enhancement training. Clients should be given the "ground-rules" of treatment, as well as an explanation of CBT. This may include a description of skills acquisition, especially drug-related skills (management of urges, dealing with high-risk situations), and general coping skills (cognitive restructuring, stress management, problem-solving skills).

It is useful to commence the intervention with feedback from assessment. Discuss the client's pattern of cannabis use, and consider the client's degree of dependence. Clients who score highly on the Severity of Dependence Scale (SDS) are often not surprised at their high level of dependence, but this fact can help to motivate them to make changes.

The main focus of the session should be on motivational enhancement training, and should cover issues such as setting goals, removing barriers to change, and identifying skills or techniques for enabling change. Behavioural self-monitoring is also a useful tool, to help the client to remain focused, or "on target", in achieving short-term goals.

Session 2

The focus is on helping the client to plan to quit. It reviews the week and homework exercises, and reviews personal triggers and high-risk situations. One of the most important skills in the first stages of quitting is coping with urges and cravings. It is also important that clients understand how to deal with slips or lapses. This information is based on the relapse prevention training model of Marlatt and Donovan (2005).

A detailed plan for quitting should be developed with the client, with a quit date set for the following week. Information and discussion of withdrawal symptoms will also be important, if only to allay fears or concerns about possible discomforts. Clients should be encouraged to examine their social support systems, and make steps to recruit appropriate persons to lend support.

Some clients will benefit from learning techniques to help them to refuse drugs, although drug refusal skills may not be necessary for all clients. Those who have relatively sophisticated communication skills will feel awkward being taught how to say "no" to a smoke.

The session should conclude with a discussion of the client's goals for the following week, and setting homework tasks.

Session 3

This session should assist the client to manage any withdrawal symptoms or problems that have arisen as a consequence of quitting in the last few days. For clients who have not quit, the problems or issues that are causing a hindrance should be addressed and resolved.

The session uses the technique of cognitive restructuring as its main focus with the main aim of assisting the client to identify when he or she is thinking negatively or engaging in automatic patterns of thought that may lead to drug use. The techniques should assist the client to interrupt this (automatic) thinking. Finally, the client should learn to challenge negative thoughts and replace them with more positive ones that help to reduce the urge to use cannabis. One theme that appears common is the process of mental "justification" for smoking, despite having decided not to smoke.

The key concept of cognitive restructuring is that thinking influences the way a person feels and behaves. Introducing the client to practical strategies for changing negative thinking is a key aspect of overcoming much of the psychological aspects of cannabis dependence. An outline of cognitive restructuring techniques is provided in the text by Jarvis, Tebbutt, Mattick, and Shand (2005).

Session 4

This session should continue the focus on cognitive strategies and begin training in further skills enhancement. After a review of the previous week's progress, determine how well the client has progressed in using thought-stopping or challenging techniques. Work with the client to overcome any problems that have arisen, and encourage the client to continue practising this skill, reminding him or her that it takes some persistence to change negative thinking.

The client should be given a choice of the personal skills to be developed in this session. These might include *problem-solving skills, management of insomnia,* or *progressive muscle relaxation* for managing stress.

Session 5

This penultimate session should focus on reviewing and consolidating the skills introduced so far, and addressing any problems that have arisen. Clients should be introduced to new skills, if these are required and time permits. This is a decision that the therapist should make based on the client's needs and progress to date. Further skills might include coping skills training, which comprises techniques such as *assertiveness skills, communication skills,* and *stress or anger management.*

Session 6

The final session should concentrate on relapse prevention and lifestyle modification issues. The main ideas to be covered include the key elements of Marlatt and Donovan's (2005) relapse prevention training.

Relapse prevention is a crucial component of treatment in the addictions. The general aim of relapse prevention training is to provide the individual with skills to avoid lapses and prevent lapses from becoming relapses to alcohol and drug use. Relapse prevention aims to help clients to learn a range of skills to avoid lapses to harmful drug or alcohol use, and to acquire behavioural strategies and changes in thinking that lessen the negative impact of a slip turning into a full-blown lapse. Relapse prevention outlines relapses as opportunities to learn rather than indications of failure.

Relapse prevention has also developed the idea that behaviour change is usually not achieved successfully in isolation – that is, individuals who are successful usually make other adjustments to their lifestyle and move towards an overall healthier and more positive way of living that complement and reinforce the initial changes in drinking or drug use.

The relapse prevention model

Successful relapse prevention and maintenance of initial change in use of alcohol or drugs is influenced to a large extent by the lifestyle of individuals. Therefore, relapse prevention training also involves examining lifestyle factors that can either hinder or support behaviour change. For example, a 25-year-old male who is single, cannabis dependent and uses heavily in social interactions may have a very different relapse prevention strategy from a married male individual whose wife does not smoke cannabis. Relapse prevention training can be divided into the following areas:

- enhancing commitment to change;
- identifying causes of relapse;
- reintroducing useful strategies;
- preparing for relapse;
- identifying lifestyle issues important to maintaining initial change.

Enhancing commitment to change

Commitment to maintaining behavioural change is an essential component in relapse prevention training. The individual may benefit from reviewing the negative aspects of drug and alcohol use and the reasons for changing their patterns.

Identifying causes of relapse

Individuals may observe that relapse occurs following a clearly identifiable event or in particular situations – for example, when the individual is anxious or depressed, has experienced a relationship breakdown, or has been under considerable social pressure to drink or take drugs. Identifying high-risk situations involves attaining information: where, when, with whom, doing what, and feeling what?

A high-risk situation is one where an individual is highly vulnerable to relapse, and one where an individual has experienced a lapse or relapse in the past. Such situations are usually laden with cues or triggers for drug use or drinking, and these have the effect of promoting urges or cravings. Such thoughts or feelings are strongly bound with the temptation to drink or use a drug, and in the absence of some alternative coping technique the client is at high risk of relapse.

High-risk situations can be grouped into three main types. Situations that feature triggers of a negative emotional nature may involve internal triggers, such as depression, stress, anxiety, or even boredom. Because these states have, in the past, reliably preceded drug use, they may be closely linked with the urge to use. Clients without adequate coping skills in such situations are at risk of relapse. Another high-risk situation involves positive mood states, which also act as internal triggers that prime a positive incentive motivational state. These situations may include celebrations or social situations, and the use of alcohol or other drugs may serve to increase the pleasant feelings involved. Finally, habitual or entrenched behavioural patterns can also prompt urges or cravings for drug or alcohol use, owing to their strong conditioned associations with past experiences. This may include an individual visiting old environments such as a local pub where drinking occurred.

Reintroducing useful strategies

Problem-solving techniques provide an effective strategy. In brief, the problem-solving process includes the following steps:

- identify the problem;
- generate a range of solutions;
- evaluate each solution;
- choose the best solution;
- decide how to put the solution into action.

Begin this component by exploring with the client his or her plans for the future, and discuss the role that smoking cannabis may or may not have in the achievement or maintenance of these goals. Help the client to beware rationalizations, as these are an important means by which clients become vulnerable to relapse. Address any possible separation loss or anxiety, such as the feeling of losing a good friend. Look at ways that the client can continue to monitor progress, to ensure that he or she remains vigilant in the future, particularly during the first few weeks after completing therapy. This can be achieved effectively by having clients record their progress.

Also consider monitoring slips or lapses, and work on strategies that will help the client to deal effectively with setbacks. The client should consider new ways of self-reward, and enjoying drug-free activities.

Finally, help the client to put the changes in a broader context, such as considering other positive lifestyle changes. Looking to the future is an important and appropriate way of concluding therapy for a serious and entrenched problem of drug dependence.

Opioids 8

Introduction

Opioids are chemicals that bind to the body's opioid receptors, that are activated by the body's "natural painkillers", such as the endorphins and enkephalins. The term *opiate* has attained a wide range of meanings over time but strictly speaking it refers to the opioids that are obtained directly from the opium poppy – morphine and codeine. However, use of the term opiate has tended to be generalized to also include heroin, which is a semi-synthetic derivative of morphine; and it has been loosely applied to a broad range of synthetic opioids that act in a similar way to morphine.

Opioid agonists are drugs that activate the opioid receptors in the same way as morphine and codeine, and include heroin as well as synthetic agonists such as methadone, levo-α-acetylmethadol (LAAM, also known as levomethadyl acetate and levacetylmethadol) and pethidine. Opioid agonists depress the activity of the central nervous system and are very effective painkillers.

Drugs that act on the opioid receptors in a way that blocks their actions are called opioid antagonists, e.g., naltrexone and naloxone. Buprenorphine is a partial agonist/antagonist that activates opioid receptors to a lesser extent than heroin and morphine while also acting to block the effects of heroin and other opioids.

Because opioid drugs such as heroin can cause overdose at relatively low doses, they are highly dangerous drugs. Their addictive liability is the second highest of all drugs of dependence, after nicotine (Anthony et al., 1994). Because they are often injected, their illicit use may lead to the transmission of blood-borne diseases such as hepatitis B and C and HIV.

The way of life among persons who are long-term daily injectors of illicit opioids is often associated with severe physical and psychological harm. In general, the dependent use of opioids is among the most damaging of all types of drug dependence. It is estimated that worldwide 226,000 people die from illicit drug use each year (Lopez et al., 2006), of which around 75% is estimated to be due to heroin use (Ridolfo & Stevenson, 2001).

Pure opioids are relatively non-toxic to living tissue and organs, a long-term opioid user given pharmaceutical supplies of pure drug is unlikely to experience the harms experienced by illicit opioid users or the liver, kidney, brain, or lung damage caused by cigarette smoking and heavy alcohol use. Historically, opioids have been used as powerful analgesics and to treat severe diarrhoea and dysentery. Despite its medical usefulness, heroin has been banned in most Western countries, and the use of morphine is restricted to those with terminal illness or severe chronic pain, such as that caused by severe injury or surgery.

Assessment

Instruments designed to assess the severity of opioid dependence include the Severity of Opiate Dependence Questionnaire (Sutherland, Edwards, Taylor, Phillips, Gossop, & Brady, 1986) and the Severity of Dependence Scale (SDS, Gossop et al., 1995). Each instrument is self-administered, and has very good reliability and validity.

The SDS is a brief five-item instrument that emphasizes the subjective aspects of drug dependence. The questions refer to an individual's concerns about stopping, anxiety about missing a dose, and perceived difficulty in stopping using the drug. A cut-off score of 4 (out of a maximum 15) has been established for heroin, amphetamine, and cannabis users (Swift et al., 1998). This instrument has proved to be very useful as a quick and informative measure of the psychological elements of drug dependence in research and clinical practice.

The Opiate Treatment Index (OPI, Darke, Ward, Hall, Heather, & Wodak, 1991) is designed to provide a standardized assessment among opioid-using clients. It is a reliable and valid instrument, incorporating basic demographics, treatment history and drug use consumption measures, assessments of HIV risk-taking behaviour, social functioning, criminality, health and psychological adjustment.

The Addiction Severity Index (ASI, McLellan et al., 1992) is one of the most commonly used standardized assessment instruments. It consists of seven sub-scales assessing previous 30-day and lifetime alcohol use, drug use, medical problems, psychiatric problems, family/social problems, employment, and legal problems. With 155 items it is rather long and a modified version has also been developed that has shown promising results (Cacciola, Alterman, McLellan, Lin, & Lynch, 2007).

Comorbid drug and mental disorders are common among those dependent on opioids, particularly post-traumatic stress disorder (Mills, Lynskey, Teesson, Ross, & Darke, 2005a; Mills, Teesson, Ross, Darke, & Shanahan, 2005b; Mills, Teesson, Ross, & Peters, 2006) and depression (Teesson et al., 2005). Comorbid disorders can influence the course and severity of the disorder and the treatment process. Thus the assessment should also probe for the coexistence of other drug and alcohol disorders and other psychiatric disorders. Brief screeners can be useful in this context, e.g., the Depression Anxiety Stress Scale (DASS, Lovibond & Lovibond, 1995); Kessler's 10 Psychological Distress Scale (K10, Kessler, 1996); Alcohol Use Disorders Identification Test (AUDIT, Saunders et al., 1993); a psychosis screener (Degenhardt et al., 2005); the Primary Care PTSD Screen (PC-PTSD, Prins et al., 2003); and the Trauma Screening Questionnaire (Brewin et al., 2002).

Interventions

Detoxification

Although detoxification is not a treatment for opioid dependence, it is an essential step towards treatment that aims to achieve abstinence (Amato, Minozzi, Davoli, Vecchi, Ferri, & Mayet, 2008; Teesson, Havard, Ross, & Darke, 2006). The opioid withdrawal syndrome is characterized by symptoms such as irritability, anxiety, pain, chills, nausea, diarrhoea, sweating, general weakness, and insomnia. These symptoms usually appear 8–12 hours after the last administration of an opioid, peak in intensity at 2–4 days after last use, and largely disappear within 7–10 days. There is a longer-term "secondary" or "protracted abstinence syndrome" of general malaise, decreased well-being, poor tolerance of stress, and a craving for the drug that may last some months. During this time opioid-dependent persons are at high risk of relapsing to opioid use.

The opioid withdrawal syndrome is not life threatening. It has been described as "immiserating", much like a bout of bad influenza that lasts about a week (Kleber, 1998). It is nonetheless sufficiently aversive for many opioid-dependent persons that it is an obstacle to abstinence that needs to be overcome humanely and effectively. Detoxification, withdrawal, or cold turkey is experienced very differently by different individuals, as these two examples of withdrawing from heroin show.

> Before my scalded eyes, the paint on the walls starts to shimmer and bubble up. Like boiled vanilla pudding. The whole world's on fire, but the flames are invisible. Their presence apparent only through sheets of heat that waft over the skin. I can't see the flames, only feel them. . . . My skin shines strawberry red. My eyes look dipped in nail polish.
>
> (Stahl, 1996, p. 93)

> Ah need some quickly. The great decline is setting in. It starts as it generally does, with a slight nausea in the pit ay ma stomach and an irrational panic attack. As soon as ah become aware ay the sickness gripping me, it effortlessly moves from the uncomfortable tae the unbearable. A toothache starts tae spread fae ma teeth intae ma jaws and ma eye sockets, and aw through ma bones in a miserable, implacable, debilitating throb. The auld sweat arrives oan cue, and let's no forget the shivers, covering ma back like a thin layer of autumn frost oan a car roof. It's time for action. No way can ah crash oot and face the music yet. Ah need the old "slowburn", a soft, come-down input. The only thing ah can move for is smack. One wee dig tae unravel those twisted limbs and send us oaf tae sleep. Then ah say goodbye to it.
>
> (Welsh, 1993, pp. 15–16)

A number of factors appear to influence rates of completion of opioid detoxification. These include the person's reasons for undertaking detoxification, and the choice of methods available to assist them. The reasons for requesting detoxification may be mixed: the person may be acting under coercion because he or she faces criminal charges; the person may be a stabilized methadone patient who chooses to withdraw from methadone treatment; the person may intend to reduce the dose of heroin required so that he or she can use it at a lower and more affordable dose; or the person may wish to become and remain abstinent.

It is often a personal crisis that precipitates the desire for detoxification (Amato et al., 2008). Apart from the physical withdrawal symptoms, there are likely to be psychological and social issues that need to be dealt with as well. A recent large review by Amato and colleagues (2008) found that psychosocial interventions such as contingency management, community reinforcement, psychological counselling and family therapy have significant impact on outcomes when added to a pharmacotherapy for detoxification from opioids. Veilleux, Colvin, Anderson, York, and Heinz (2010) also emphasize the importance of employing psychological interventions alongside pharmacotherapy for opioid detoxification. As they point out, detoxification is often the first contact of people with opioid dependence with the healthcare system. Psychosocial support provided at this time can increase future treatment contact and outcomes.

Pharmacological interventions that can assist detoxification include the opioids methadone and buprenorphine, and the α_2-adrenergic agonists, clonidine and lofexidine. Methadone-assisted withdrawal by tapering methadone doses is an effective method of achieving opioid withdrawal over a period of a week to 10 days (Amato, Davoli, Minozzi, Ali, & Ferri, 2005). Clonidine and lofexidine are more effective than placebo in managing withdrawal from heroin and methadone (Gowing, Farrell, Ali, & White, 2009c). Buprenorphine is more effective than clonidine or lofexidine, and may be more effective than methadone, especially in inpatient settings (Gowing, Ali, & White, 2009a).

Withdrawal from opioids can be accelerated by using the opioid antagonist naltrexone. This method intensifies acute opioid withdrawal symptoms and has generally been unacceptable to dependent opioid users without sedation. Light sedation (use of clonidine or lofexidine) makes this method of withdrawal more acceptable to patients (Gowing, Ali, & White, 2009b). Managing opioid withdrawal in this way is feasible but Gowing et al. found that research on the value of the procedure was of poor quality. The use of ultra-rapid detoxification with naltrexone (UROD), where anaesthesia is used to ease the process of withdrawal (Gowing, Ali, & White, 2010), is not recommended because of its potential risks and high costs.

Several studies have found that more opioid-dependent patients complete inpatient than outpatient detoxification (Day, Ison, &

Strang, 2005; Mattick & Hall, 1996). The interpretation of these results is complicated, however, by the fact that the location of detoxification (outpatient or inpatient) has been confounded by the intensity of intervention, that is, patients in inpatient settings receive much more psychosocial and other support than patients in outpatient settings. It is also likely that many opioid-dependent persons live in settings that are unsupportive of detoxification and abstinence (e.g., with other opioid users), and hence are less likely to complete outpatient than inpatient detoxification.

While detoxification is not a treatment for opioid dependence, it is the first step in an abstinence-oriented treatment (Mattick & Hall, 1996). People who have undergone detoxification are no less likely to relapse to drug use than those who have not (Gerstein & Harwood, 1990; Simpson & Sells, 1982; Teesson et al., 2006). In the absence of additional support and treatment most opioid-dependent persons will relapse to opioid use after detoxification (Mattick & Hall, 1996).

Detoxification is more appropriately regarded as a process that aims to achieve a safe and humane withdrawal from a drug of dependence. The criteria for assessing its effectiveness are accordingly the rates of completion of the process, and the severity of withdrawal symptoms and distress that drug-dependent persons experience during it. Detoxification also provides opioid-dependent people with a period of respite from their drug use and its consequences, an opportunity to reflect on the wisdom of continued drug use, and an opportunity to take up offers of intervention. Detoxification can thus be a prelude to more specific forms of drug-free treatment for opioid dependence.

Drug-free treatment approaches

Drug-free treatment approaches include residential treatment in therapeutic communities (TCs), self-help groups such as Narcotics Anonymous (NA), and outpatient drug counselling. TCs and NA share a commitment to achieving abstinence from opioid and other illicit drugs; they do not involve the substitution of opioid drugs for heroin; and they typically use group and psychological interventions to assist heroin users to remain abstinent and address their personal problems in ways other than by using opioids. Drug counselling can occur with or without the concurrent use of pharmacotherapies.

TCs typically involve residential programmes of 3–12 months in length. During this time, ex-users live and work within a community of other ex-users and professional staff (some of whom are "recovered addicts"). Group processes and individual counselling are used to change self-defeating behaviour and to support abstinence (Mattick & Hall, 1993). Because drug-free treatments are ideologically opposed to pharmacotherapies, it is difficult to carry out randomized controlled trials comparing the two modalities. People self-select into the form of treatment that best suits their beliefs and those of significant others.

Research on TCs usually involves comparing different types of TCs or TCs with community residence. A review from the Cochrane Collaboration found seven robust studies on TCs and concluded that "there is little evidence that TCs offer significant benefits in comparison with other residential treatment, or that one type of TC is better than another. Prison TC may be better than prison on its own or Mental Health Treatment Programmes to prevent re-offending post-release for inmates" (Smith, Gates, & Foxcroft, 2006, p. 2).

Drug-free counselling is usually provided individually on an outpatient basis by drug counsellors (usually professionals, but it may include some former drug users). The aim is to address any underlying psychological problems and to assist drug users to become and remain abstinent. These programmes often provide vocational rehabilitation and training. A review of psychosocial treatment alone for heroin abuse and dependence found that there is not sufficient research evidence to support such interventions nor to show they are superior to other forms of treatment (Mayet, Farrell, Ferri, Amato, & Davoli, 2004).

In general, TC and counselling programmes do achieve substantial reductions in heroin use and crime among the minority of entrants who remain in treatment for long enough to benefit (at least 3 months) (Gerstein & Harwood, 1990; Hubbard, Craddock, Flynn, Anderson, & Etheridge, 1997; Mattick & Hall, 1993; Shanahan, Havard, Teesson, Mills, Williamson, & Ross, 2006; Teesson et al., 2008).

NA runs self-help groups in the community that follow a programme modelled on the 12-step approach originally developed by AA. Such programmes assume that addiction is a disease for which there is no cure and that recovery can only occur if the person remains abstinent from all mind-altering substances. The fellowship assists its members to achieve and maintain abstinence by providing mutual help and support in working through the structured programme of the 12 steps. There is no good research evidence on the effectiveness of NA, although there is reasonable evidence for the value of AA in supporting abstinence from alcohol.

Pharmacotherapies

Pharmacotherapies for heroin are also referred to as "substitution" treatments because one opioid is substituted for the illicit opioids. The substituted drug is usually a longer-acting opioid, e.g., methadone, buprenorphine, or LAAM. There has been considerable controversy over this type of drug substitution, with critics claiming that the process simply replaces one drug of abuse with another. A review by Gerra and colleagues (2009) demonstrated that there are sufficient differential effects of the substituted drugs from those of heroin to refer to them as "maintenance agents" or "long-acting opioid agonists" rather than the more pejorative term "substitution agents". They act as a medication for heroin addiction by reducing craving and controlling addictive behaviour.

Methadone

The oldest and most widely used maintenance agent is methadone. Methadone has the advantages that it is long-acting and effective when taken orally. This means that a client of a methadone programme requires only one dose per day, instead of the two or three injections required by a heroin-dependent individual. The oral route of administration also substantially reduces the risks of injecting opioids. Larger methadone doses of between 60 and 100 mg or more per day are more effective in retaining clients in treatment and reducing illicit opioid use than are lower doses (Hall & Mattick, 2007).

Methadone maintenance was pioneered by Dole and Nyswander in New York in the early 1960s (Dole & Nyswander, 1965). They argued that opioid addiction resembled a metabolic illness, such as diabetes. Just as a diabetic requires regular injections of insulin to maintain normal functioning, so people who are dependent on opioids required administration of an opioid. Most people dependent on opioids, they suggested, have either an innate or acquired deficiency in endogenous opioids (the natural opioids of the brain that are involved in pain regulation). A daily dose of methadone restores this deficiency and maintains the level of opioids at a stable level throughout the day.

While the metabolic theory of opioid dependence has not been supported, the evidence strongly supports methadone as a method of managing opioid dependence (Mattick, Breen, Kimber, & Davoli, 2009). Methadone maintenance treatment reduces heroin and cocaine use, infectious disease transmission, damage to veins and skin infections, criminal activity, psychological problems, and social problems

(Ward, Mattick, & Hall, 1998). Methadone does not entirely eliminate the illicit use of opioids, nor the use of other illicit drugs, such as cocaine and cannabis, which are often abused by methadone clients. However, the use of illicit opioids is substantially reduced by methadone maintenance treatment (Mattick et al., 2009; Ward et al., 1998).

Methadone maintenance treatment blocks the euphoric effects of heroin and other opioids while preventing the onset of withdrawal. It stabilizes patients, allowing them to benefit from psychosocial rehabilitation. It is a well-accepted intervention for opioid dependence, and is widely used in Australia, parts of Europe, the USA, and the UK (Hall & Mattick, 2007). People who are dependent on heroin have an improved quality of life when taking methadone:

> A 24-year-old single woman presents for treatment for her heroin problem. Two weeks before she had been disciplined and given notice in her job due to lateness. She was resolved to keep her job. She began a methadone programme and after an initial period of daily attendance for dose titration, she was stabilized on methadone.

Alternative maintenance treatments

Buprenorphine

Buprenorphine is a mixed agonist–antagonist: it has partial agonist effects similar to those of morphine but less powerful, while blocking the effects of pure agonists such as heroin or morphine. Buprenorphine requires less frequent dosage than methadone – usually every 2 days at doses of 8–15 mg. This permits buprenorphine to be administered every 2 or 3 days, increasing flexibility for the client and reducing demands on the clinic. There is also a lower risk of overdose from buprenorphine than with methadone, and buprenorphine withdrawal is shorter and less intense than methadone.

Mattick, Kimber, Breen, and Davoli (2008) reviewed the research on efficacy of buprenorphine and found it improved treatment outcome and illicit opioid use compared with placebo when administered in medium (8–15 mg) to high (16 mg) doses. It was less effective than methadone administered in doses of 60 mg to 120 mg a day. It was therefore recommended that methadone be the treatment of first choice in most clinical settings (Hall & Mattick, 2007).

Levo-α-acetylmethadol

Levo-α-acetylmethadol (LAAM) is a longer acting form of methadone with a duration of action of 48 to 72 hours. A large-scale review of efficacy research found it superior to methadone (Clark et al., 2002), but it has been withdrawn from use because of case reports of cardiac arrhythmias (Hall & Mattick, 2007).

Heroin prescription

Injectable heroin has been prescribed for dependent heroin users for whom oral maintenance treatments are not effective. A summary of research found that the few studies that have been completed showed inconsistent methods and conflicting results (Ferri, Davoli, & Perucci Carlo, 2010). Ferri et al. point out that there are new heroin maintenance programmes starting up in several countries, results from which should better inform decisions regarding the efficacy of heroin prescription and the characteristics of the patients who respond best to it.

Codeine

Another drug that has been trialled for the treatment of opioid dependence is codeine. Although research is in its early stages, Hall and Mattick (2007) suggested that it had potential to be used as a cheap and effective alternative to other oral maintenance treatments.

Naltrexone

Naltrexone blocks the opioid receptors, displacing any opioids in a person's system and blocking the effects of opioid agonists. Naltrexone must be taken daily as a maintenance drug so one of the biggest determinants of its effectiveness is the client's motivation to remain abstinent and to take the drug. Such motivation may not characterize the majority of opioid-dependent persons who enter treatment under some form of coercion (either legal or social). In such patients treated with naltrexone, over 90% will resume illicit opioid use within 12 months in the absence of other treatment (Kosten, 1990).

The success of naltrexone maintenance also depends on the type of treatment programme and the nature of the client group (Stine & Kosten, 1997). For example, the majority of business executives and physicians who are opioid dependent and are prescribed naltrexone in combination with outpatient treatment significantly improve their social and professional functioning and most remain opioid-free (Gold, Dackis, & Washton, 1984; Ling & Wesson, 1984; Roth, Hogan,

& Farren, 1997; Washton, Gold, & Pottash, 1984). By comparison, a study of illicit opioid-dependent persons with an average length of 10.5 years of dependence found only 17% remained in treatment after 90 days, despite all expressing a desire to achieve abstinence (Rawson & Tennant, 1984).

Recent large-scale reviews have concluded that highly motivated individuals are most likely to benefit from naltrexone maintenance treatment. A review of oral naltrexone (Minozzi, Amato, Vecchi, Davoli, Kirchmayer, & Verster, 2006) concluded that there is insufficient good quality research to assess the effectiveness of naltrexone maintenance. When naltrexone is compared with placebo, findings were non-significant, but where psychosocial treatment was added to naltrexone and placebo, naltrexone was superior in terms of heroin use during treatment. There were no advantages for naltrexone over other treatments in terms of retention in treatment, side effects or relapse at follow-up. Naltrexone when combined with psychosocial therapy was more effective than psychosocial treatment alone in studies of prison parolees or probationers (Minozzi et al., 2011). These studies were from diverse countries and used varying dose schedules for naltrexone, making it hard to specify the characteristics of effective treatment.

Sustained release depot injections and implants have recently been investigated as a way of improving compliance. A review of research on sustained-release naltrexone found that there was insufficient evidence to evaluate its effects (Lobmaier, Kornor, Kunoe, & Bjørndal, 2008), and that administration site adverse effects were common. They concluded that more research was needed, particularly providing more data on these adverse side effects. Two small randomized controlled trials have since been completed – one comparing naltrexone implant to oral naltrexone (Kunoe et al., 2009). Both of these trials found the naltrexone implant more effective in preventing relapse to heroin use than the comparison (control) condition during the course of the trials. However, longer-term outcomes are less clear. Both studies concluded that the implant procedure was relatively safe.

Summary

Heroin dependence is one of the most serious types of drug dependence in terms of persistence, elevated mortality rate, and increased psychological and physical morbidity.

Completion of opioid withdrawal is not life threatening but it can be immiserating and an obstacle to the achievement of abstinence. Opioid withdrawal can be completed using methadone and buprenorphine, and the α_2-adrenergic agonists clonidine and lofexidine, and naltrexone given under light sedation. The effectiveness of these pharmacotherapies is enhanced by psychosocial support. Detoxification is not a treatment for opioid dependence *per se*. Without follow-up treatment and support, most heroin-dependent persons will return to heroin use after completing withdrawal.

Drug-free forms of treatment that aim to achieve enduring abstinence from opioids include TCs, drug-free counselling, and self-help groups such as NA. Drug-free approaches are not attractive to many users and have modest rates of retention but are of considerable benefit to the minority of patients who remain in them for 3 months or more.

The major form of treatment for opioid dependence in Australia, the UK, Europe and the USA has been methadone maintenance treatment. This involves maintaining heroin-dependent people on the long-acting oral opioid methadone, usually given daily under supervision. This stabilizes the person's opioid use and makes him or her more accessible to psychological and social interventions. It has been shown to substantially reduce heroin use and crime and to improve the health and well-being of heroin-dependent people while in treatment. An alternative effective form of maintenance drug is buprenorphine (a mixed agonist–antagonist drug). The opioid antagonist naltrexone has much lower rates of retention but may be of use in more highly motivated patients and those whose compliance can be supervised, such as opioid-dependent health professionals.

In the interests of increasing patient choice and the attractiveness of treatment, a number of alternative maintenance agents have been investigated. These include LAAM, an opioid agonist that has been found to be very effective, but has been withdrawn from use due to serious side effects. Others under investigation, which are also showing promise for some types of opioid-dependent patients, are heroin prescription and codeine maintenance.

Psychostimulants: cocaine, amphetamines and ecstasy 9

Introduction

The most commonly used psychostimulant drugs are cocaine, meth-amphetamine, and ecstasy (European Commission, Trimbos Institute, & RAND Europe, 2009). Cocaine is obtained from the coca leaf, which is native to parts of South America. The amphetamines are synthetic drugs of which there are three main forms: amphetamine, dexamphetamine and methamphetamine. Ecstasy is a derivative of amphetamine that has hallucinogenic as well as stimulant properties.

Methamphetamine is the more potent form of amphetamine. The initial product of synthesis is methamphetamine base, which is a yellow or brown liquid. This is converted to a (more bioaccessible) water-soluble salt by mixing with an acid. The salt can be in the form of a powder of varying strength and colour (speed), or a clear crystal (ice) that is the most refined form of methamphetamine.

Since the early 1990s, the use of cocaine has declined in North America, which nonetheless remains the largest market for cocaine. Its use has been increasing in the rest of the world, however, par-ticularly in Western and Central Europe and South America. Over this same period, use of methamphetamines and ecstasy has risen rapidly in developed and developing countries, especially in Asia and in the Near and Middle East (UNODC, 2009).

Psychostimulants can be swallowed, snorted, smoked, or injected. Ecstasy is usually available as a pill, which is swallowed. Cocaine is snorted or smoked ("crack" cocaine). The more purified form of methamphetamine ("crystal meth" or "ice") is most commonly smoked or injected. Administration by injection adds significantly to the risks associated with using these drugs, such as fatal overdose, a paranoid psychosis, and dependence (Darke, Kaye, McKetin, & Duflou, 2008).

Assessment

A non-confrontational, empathic, and mutually respectful therapeutic relationship is more likely to engage those more entrenched patients who are unwilling to accept that they have a problem (Britt, Hudson, & Blampied, 2004; Platt, 1997). In assessing the patient, the therapist should obtain the patient's history of drug use, including where, how, and why the stimulant has been used. He or she should also obtain a psychiatric history and any information about psychiatric symptoms related to stimulant use. Finally, it should include a thorough physical examination, including urinalysis.

There are general measures that have been found to be useful in assessing psychostimulant dependence prior to treatment. For example, measures of readiness to change such as the Readiness to Change Questionnaire (Budd & Rollnick, 1997), the Readiness Ruler (Hesse, 2006), SOCRATES (Stages of Change Readiness and Treatment Eagerness Scale, Miller & Tonigan, 1996) and URICA (University of Rhode Island Change Assessment, Callaghan et al., 2005; Pantalon, Nich, Frankforter, Carroll, & University of Rhode Island Change, 2002) may assist the clinician to assess patients' attitudes towards their drug problems and provide a basis for motivating behaviour change. The Severity of Dependence Scale has also been found to be a useful brief measure of psychostimulant dependence and associated problems (Bruno, Matthews, Topp, Degenhardt, Gomez, & Dunn, 2009; Gossop et al., 1995; Topp & Mattick, 1997).

Other standard self-report questionnaires are available that have been designed specifically for the assessment of cocaine abuse. The Voris Cocaine Craving Scale (Smelson, McGee, Caulfield, Bergstein, & Engelhart, 1999) and the Drug Impairment Rating Scale (Halikas, Crosby, & Nugent, 1992; Halikas, Nugent, Crosby, & Carlson, 1993) both have good reliability and validity in assessing self-reported impairment, both for initial assessment and treatment outcome measurement. Kampman et al. (1998) developed the Cocaine Selective Severity Assessment (CSSA) – a scale to measure the symptoms of early cocaine withdrawal. They found the instrument to have good reliability and validity and to be clinically useful in predicting early treatment failure. A scale derived from the CSSA specifically for use with the assessment of withdrawal from amphetamine abuse has recently been developed and demonstrates good reliability and validity (McGregor, Srisurapanont, Mitchell, Longo, Cahill, & White, 2008).

An adaptation of the Scale for Assessment of Positive Symptoms in psychosis has been developed to assess the nature and severity of psychotic symptoms in cocaine dependence (The Scale for Assessment of Positive Symptoms for Cocaine-Induced Psychosis (SAPS-CIP) (Cubells et al., 2005)). This scale is a useful tool in treatment planning for cocaine users and is likely to prove helpful in assessing psychotic symptoms in psychostimulant users more generally.

Psychostimulant abuse often occurs comorbidly with other psychiatric disorders such as depression, anxiety, and personality disorders, as well as with other drug use disorders (Ford et al., 2009). It is therefore recommended that other psychiatric and drug use disorders are included in the assessment process to inform treatment planning. Whether the drug use preceded the psychiatric disorder is also relevant to treatment planning (Mills et al., 2009). Brief psychiatric screeners such as the Kessler 10 Psychiatric Distress Scale (Kessler, 1996), and the Depression, Anxiety, Stress Scale (Lovibond & Lovibond, 1995) can be used to ascertain initial comorbidity status and screen for other complicating psychiatric disorders (Mills et al., 2009).

Interventions

Intervention for psychostimulant disorders usually involves an initial step of detoxification where the patient withdraws from all drug use. A period of treatment aimed at supporting abstinence then follows.

Detoxification

Detoxification from cocaine appears to result in relatively low-level withdrawal symptoms (Walsh, Stoops, Moody, Lin, & Bigelow, 2009). In their review of the literature, Proudfoot and Teesson (2000) concluded that medication was not recommended in assisting individuals to withdraw from cocaine. Withdrawal from amphetamines has been identified as a barrier to reducing their use; but a recent Cochrane Collaboration review of medications for use in assisting amphetamine withdrawal concluded that no medication has been identified that assists in this process (Shoptaw, Kao, Heinzerling, & Ling, 2009). The findings for the drug mirtazipine were equivocal, and the authors concluded that further research may be beneficial on this and similar types of drugs that act to increase the activity of dopamine, noradrenaline (norepinephrine), or serotonin in the central nervous system.

Pharmacotherapies

Depression is often associated with the use of and withdrawal from psychostimulants; consequently, a large number of studies have evaluated the effectiveness of antidepressants in treating psychostimulant abuse. Recent systematic reviews carried out for the Cochrane Collaboration have found little support for these pharmacotherapies, although drugs such as desipramine, imipramine and fluoxetine have shown some promise in individual trials treating cocaine or amphetamine abuse (Minozzi et al., 2008; Srisurapanont, Jarusuraisin, & Kittirattanapaiboon, 2008). Reviews of the effectiveness of anticonvulsants (Minozzi et al., 2008), antipsychotic medications (Amato, Minozzi, Pani, & Davoli, 2007), and dopamine agonists have found little or no support for these pharmacotherapies, although a trial of modafinil, a dopamine agonist that also improves mood, has shown promise (Shearer et al., 2009). Given the wide range of pharmacotherapies assessed in the research literature, one panel of reviewers suggests that it would be a better use of research money and time if focus was made on those drugs that have to date shown some limited promise of efficacy (Minozzi et al., 2008).

Although some drug treatments have shown promise, further research is clearly warranted. Various reviewers have suggested that such research should trial combinations of psychosocial support for retention in treatment with pharmacotherapy (Proudfoot & Teesson, 2000; Minozzi et al., 2008; Srisurapanont et al., 2008).

Psychological techniques

Psychological interventions have similar (low) levels of research support as pharmacological treatments for psychostimulant use. Again there are promising areas of research, but little that can be firmly recommended (Knapp, Soares, Farrell, & Silva de Lima, 2007). Perhaps the most exciting developments over recent years is the growing support for contingency management, which usually involves an exchange of vouchers for negative urine samples

(Cameron & Ritter, 2007; Knapp et al., 2007; Petry, Alessi, & Hanson, 2007). Treatment agencies can experience problems in funding the costs of vouchers in such programmes. Research from Australia suggests that a brief cognitive behavioural intervention can have beneficial outcomes provided the patients attend at least two sessions of treatment (Baker et al., 2005).

There is little demand for treatment by ecstasy users and limited published research on the efficacy of treatments for ecstasy problems. The status of ecstasy dependence as a diagnosis is uncertain (Degenhardt et al., 2010a). As with other psychostimulants, the best recommendation for treatment is contingency management. Cognitive behavioural therapy may also prove helpful.

Summary

Although there is a considerable body of research on cocaine abuse, there is a paucity of good research on assessment and treatments for amphetamines, which is increasing in prevalence in many parts of the world. Further research on pharmacotherapies for psychostimulant abuse needs to assess complementary psychosocial and pharmacological therapies and demonstrate that specific pharmacotherapies add to overall treatment effectiveness. The safety of psychostimulant use is unpredictable and, given the poor retention rates achieved in this area of research, caution should be exercised when trialling new medications because of the possibility of additive negative effects of the trial drug and psychostimulants. Drugs that address the co-occurring depression of psychostimulant users appear to show greater efficacy among the pharmacotherapies. Contingency management and brief CBT have shown the most promise among the psychological treatments studied.

Addiction: Looking ahead 10

Where should our efforts in research and understanding of drug use and addiction be directed? At the beginning of this book we set out to answer the two following questions.

1 Why do some people develop problems with alcohol and drugs and others do not?
2 How do we respond to these problems?

These are complex and intriguing questions with no simple answers. Addiction is determined by a multiple of interacting factors, the unravelling of which presents a major research challenge for the future. It is clear that genetic and environmental factors can play significant roles in initiation and maintenance of drug use. It is also clear that learning within a sociocultural context is important and that changing this context can be a way of treating drug and alcohol problems.

There is little doubt that the addictions cause a considerable burden to society. Global Burden of Disease studies have confirmed that alcohol and tobacco are major contributors to the burden of disease in developed countries, and they are increasingly becoming so in developing countries (Lopez et al., 2006; Mohapatra, Patra, Popova, Duhig, & Rehm, 2010). The extent of the burden remains to be clearly outlined for the illicit drugs individually, although research is now underway to provide this information (e.g., Degenhardt, Calabria, Hall, & Lynskey, 2008).

Motivational factors and individual preference for treatment type are important factors in determining treatment effectiveness. We need a better understanding of the impact of comorbid psychological and physical illnesses. Assessing and effectively treating these comorbid disorders has led to improved outcomes in drug and alcohol treatment. In general, a stepped care approach is recommended where less intensive interventions are used before more costly psychological and medical interventions.

The illegality of some drugs of addiction will continue to present both moral and logistical issues in our response. In particular, the use of illicit drugs for the treatment of dependence remains a challenge in the addictions. For example, there has been considerable controversy over the use of injectable heroin for those people for whom other treatments are ineffective. However, research continues to be carried out on this treatment because of the significant need of the chronically heroin-dependent people in our communities.

What of the future? A growing understanding of the neurobiology of alcohol and drug addiction may lead to new and better pharmacological treatments of alcohol and other drug dependence. The use of illicit drugs by young people in the developed world will probably continue to prompt investment in basic science and efforts to translate scientific advances into effective treatment. The challenge is to incorporate new pharmacological treatments within a public health approach to alcohol and other drug use. A combination of biological and social perspectives on drug use and addiction is required if we are substantially to reduce the burden of disease and disability produced by alcohol and other drug use (Hall, 1997).

Further reading

Baker, A., & Velleman, R. (Eds.) (2007). *Clinical handbook of co-existing mental health and drug and alcohol problems.* New York: Routledge.

Brady, K. T., Back, S. E., & Greenfield, S. F. (Eds.). (2009). *Women and addiction: A comprehensive textbook.* New York: Guilford Press.

Hall, W., & Degenhardt, L. (2009). The adverse health effects of nonmedical cannabis use. *Lancet, 374,* 1383–1391.

Hall, W., & Pacula, R. L. (2003). *Cannabis use and dependence: Public health and public policy.* Melbourne: Cambridge University Press.

References

Abbot, N. C., Stead, L. F., White, A. R., Barnes, J., & Ernst, E. (2000). Hypnotherapy for smoking cessation. *Cochrane Database of Systematic Reviews*, 2, CD001008.

Agosti, V., & Levin, F. R. (2004). Predictors of treatment contact among individuals with cannabis dependence. *American Journal of Drug & Alcohol Abuse, 30* (1), 121–127.

Ainslie, G. (1992). *Picoeconomics*. Cambridge: Cambridge University Press.

Ait-Daoud, N., Malcolm, R. J., Jr., & Johnson, B. A. (2006). An overview of medications for the treatment of alcohol withdrawal and alcohol dependence with an emphasis on the use of older and newer anticonvulsants. *Addictive Behaviors, 31* (9), 1628–1649.

Allen, N. E., Beral, V., Casabonne, D., Kan, S. W., Reeves, G. K., Brown, A., et al. (2009). Moderate alcohol intake and cancer incidence in women. *Journal of the National Cancer Institute, 101* (5), 296–305.

Alonso, J., Angermeyer, M. C., Bernert, S., Bruffaerts, R., Brugha, T. S., Bryson, H., et al. (2004). Prevalence of mental disorders in Europe: Results from the European Study of the Epidemiology of Mental Disorders (ESEMeD) project. *Acta Psychiatrica Scandinavica, 109* (Suppl. 420), 21–27.

Alterman, A. I., Hayashida, M., & O'Brien, C. P. (1988). Treatment response and safety of ambulatory medical detoxification. *Journal of Studies on Alcohol, 49* (2), 160–166.

Altman, J., Everitt, B., Glautier, S., Markou, A., Nutt, D., Oretti, R., et al. (1996). The biological, social and clinical bases of drug addiction: Commentary and debate. *Psychopharmacology, 125,* 285–345.

Alwyn, T., John, B., Hodgson, R. J., & Phillips, C. J. (2004). The addition of a psychological intervention to a home detoxification programme. *Alcohol & Alcoholism, 39* (6), 536–541.

Amato, L., Davoli, M., Minozzi, S., Ali, R., & Ferri, M. (2005). Methadone at tapered doses for the management of opioid withdrawal. *Cochrane Database of Systematic Reviews, 3,* CD003409. Retrieved June 3, 2011, from http://www2.cochrane.org/reviews/en/ab003409.html

Amato, L., Minozzi, S., Davoli, M., Vecchi, S., Ferri, M., & Mayet, S. (2008). Psychosocial and pharmacological treatments versus pharmacological treatments for opioid detoxification. *Cochrane Database of Systematic Reviews, 4,* CD005031. Retrieved June 3, 2011, from http://www2.cochrane.org/reviews/en/ab005031.html

Amato, L., Minozzi, S., Pani, P. P., &

Davoli, M. (2007). Antipsychotic medications for cocaine dependence. *Cochrane Database of Systematic Reviews*, 4, CD006306. Retrieved June 3, 2011, from http://www2.cochrane.org/reviews/en/ab005031.html

American Psychiatric Association. (1994). *Diagnostic and statistical manual of mental disorders* (4th edition). Washington, DC: American Psychiatric Association.

American Psychiatric Association. (2010). *DSM-5 Development*. Washington, DC: American Psychiatric Association. Retrieved June 3, 2011, from http://www.dsm5.org/ProposedRevisions/Pages/Substance-RelatedDisorders.aspx

Anda, R., Williamson, D., Escobedo, L., Mast, E., Giovino, G., & Remington, P. (1990). Depression and the dynamics of smoking. *Journal of the American Medical Association*, 264 (12), 1541–1545.

Andrews, G., Hall, W. D., Teesson, M., & Henderson, S. (1999). *The mental health of Australians*. Canberra: Mental Health Branch, Commonwealth Department of Health and Aged Care.

Annis, H. M., & Graham, J. M. (1988). *Situational Confidence Questionnaire (SCQ) user' guide*. Toronto: ARF.

Anthony, J., & Helzer, J. E. (1991). Syndromes of drug abuse and dependence. In L. N. Robins, & D. A. Reiger (Eds.), *Psychiatric disorders in America* (p. 116). New York: Free Press.

Anthony, J. C., Warner, L., & Kessler, R. (1994). Comparative epidemiology of dependence on tobacco, alcohol, controlled substances, and inhalants: Basic findings from the National Comorbidity Survey. *Experimental and Clinical Psychopharmacology*, 2 (3), 244–268.

Arendt, M., Rosenberg, R., Foldager, L., Perto, G., & Munk-Jorgensen, P. (2007). Psychopathology among cannabis-dependent treatment seekers and association with later substance abuse treatment. *Journal of Substance Abuse Treatment*, 32 (2), 113–119.

Assanangkornchai, S., & Srisurapanont, M. (2007). The treatment of alcohol dependence. *Current Opinion in Psychiatry*, 20 (3), 222–227.

Australian Bureau of Statistics. (2008). *National Survey of Mental Health and Wellbeing: Summary of results, 2007*. Canberra: Australian Bureau of Statistics. Retrieved June 3, 2011, from http://www.abs.gov.au/ausstats/ABS@.nsf/Latestproducts/4326.0Main%20Features12007?opendocument&tabname=Summary&prodno=4326.0&issue=2007&num=&view=

Azrin, N. H., Acierno, R., Kogan, E. S., Donohue, B., Besalel, V. A., & McMahon, P. T. (1996). Follow-up results of supportive versus behavioral therapy for illicit drug use. *Behaviour Research & Therapy*, 34 (1), 41–46.

Babor, T. F., Higgins-Biddle, J. C., Saunders, J. B., & Monteiro, M. G. (2001). *AUDIT: The alcohol use disorder identification test* (2nd ed.). Geneva: World Health Organization.

Baker, A., Lee, N. K., Claire, M., Lewin, T. J., Grant, T., Pohlman, S., et al. (2005). Brief cognitive behavioural interventions for regular amphetamine users: A step in the right direction. *Addiction*, 100 (3), 367–378.

Bala, M., & Lesniak, W. (2007). Efficacy of non-pharmacological methods used for treating tobacco dependence: Meta-analysis. *Polskie Archiwum Medycyny Wewnetrznej*, 117 (11–12), 504–511.

Bala, M., Lesniak, W., & Strzeszynski, L. (2008a). Efficacy of pharmacological methods used for treating tobacco dependence: Meta-analysis. *Polskie Archiwum Medycyny Wewnetrznej*, 118 (1–2), 20–28.

Bala, M., Strzeszynski, L., & Cahill, K. (2008b). Mass media interventions for smoking cessation in adults. *Cochrane Database of Systematic Reviews*, 1,

CD004704. Retrieved June 3, 2011, from http://www2.cochrane.org/reviews/en/ab004704.html

Balk, E., Lynskey, M. T., & Agrawal, A. (2009). The association between DSM-IV nicotine dependence and stressful life events in the National Epidemiologic Survey on Alcohol and Related Conditions. *American Journal of Drug and Alcohol Abuse, 35* (2), 85–90.

Barth, J., Critchley, J., & Bengel, J. (2008). Psychosocial interventions for smoking cessation in patients with coronary heart disease. *Cochrane Database of Systematic Reviews, 1,* CD006886. Retrieved June 3, 2011, from http://www2.cochrane.org/reviews/en/ab006886.html

Becker, G. S., & Murphy, K. M. (1988). A theory of rational addiction. *Journal of Political Economy, 96,* 675–700.

Begg, S., Vos, T., Barker, B., Stevenson, C., Stanley, L., & Lopez, A. (2007). *The burden of disease and injury in Australia 2003.* Canberra: Australian Institute of Health and Welfare.

Benowitz, N. L. (2008). Neurobiology of nicotine addiction: Implications for smoking cessation treatment. *American Journal of Medicine, 121* (4 Suppl 1), S3–10.

Benyamina, A., Lecacheux, M., Blecha, L., Reynaud, M., & Lukasiewcz, M. (2008). Pharmacotherapy and psychotherapy in cannabis withdrawal and dependence. *Expert Review of Neurotherapeutics, 8* (3), 479–491.

Bierut, L. J., Dinwiddie, S. H., Begleiter, H., Crowe, R. R., Hesselbrock, V., Nurnberger, J. I., Jr., et al. (1998). Familial transmission of substance dependence: Alcohol, marijuana, cocaine, and habitual smoking: A report from the Collaborative Study on the Genetics of Alcoholism. *Archives of General Psychiatry, 55* (11), 982–988.

Bijl, R. V., Ravelli, A., & van Zessen, G. (1998). Prevalence of psychiatric disorder in the general population: Results of the Netherlands Mental Health Survey and Incidence Study (NEMESIS). *Social Psychiatry and Psychiatric Epidemiology, 33* (12), 587–595.

Bischof, G., Grothues, J. M., Reinhardt, S., Meyer, C., John, U., & Rumpf, H.-J. (2008). Evaluation of a telephone-based stepped care intervention for alcohol-related disorders: a randomized controlled trial. *Drug & Alcohol Dependence, 93* (3), 244–251.

Bize, R., Burnand, B., Mueller, Y., & Cornuz, J. (2007). Effectiveness of biomedical risk assessment as an aid for smoking cessation: A systematic review. *Tobacco Control, 16* (3), 151–156.

Bradley, K. A., DeBenedetti, A. F., Volk, R. J., Williams, E. C., Frank, D., & Kivlahan, D. R. (2007). AUDIT-C as a brief screen for alcohol misuse in primary care. *Alcoholism: Clinical & Experimental Research, 31* (7), 1208–1217.

Brewin, C. R., Rose, S., Andrews, B., Green, J., Tata, P., McEvedy, C., et al. (2002). Brief screening instrument for post-traumatic stress disorder. *British Journal of Psychiatry, 181,* 158–162.

Britt, E., Hudson, S. M., & Blampied, N. M. (2004). Motivational interviewing in health settings: A review. *Patient Education & Counseling, 53* (2), 147–155.

Brook, J. S., Whiteman, M., Gordon, A., & Brook, D. (1988). The role of older brothers in younger brothers' drug use viewed in the context of parent and peer influences. *Journal of Genetic Psychology, 151,* 59–75.

Brown, R. L., Saunders, L. A., Bobula, J. A., Mundt, M. P., & Koch, P. E. (2007). Randomized-controlled trial of a telephone and mail intervention for alcohol use disorders: Three-month drinking outcomes. *Alcoholism: Clinical & Experimental Research, 31* (8), 1372–1379.

Bruno, R., Matthews, A. J., Topp, L.,

Degenhardt, L., Gomez, R., & Dunn, M. (2009). Can the Severity of Dependence Scale be usefully applied to 'ecstasy'? *Neuropsychobiology, 60,* 137–147.

Budd, R. J., & Rollnick, S. (1997). The structure of the Readiness to Change Questionnaire: A test of Prochaska & DiClemente's transtheoretical model. *British Journal of Health Psychology, 2* (Part 4), 365–376.

Budney, A. J., & Hughes, J. R. (2006). The cannabis withdrawal syndrome. *Current Opinion in Psychiatry, 19* (3), 233–238.

Cacciola, J. S., Alterman, A. I., McLellan, A. T., Lin, Y.-T., & Lynch, K. G. (2007). Initial evidence for the reliability and validity of a "Lite" version of the Addiction Severity Index. *Drug & Alcohol Dependence, 87* (2–3), 297–302.

Cahill, K., Moher, M., & Lancaster, T. (2008a). Workplace interventions for smoking cessation. *Cochrane Database of Systematic Reviews, 4,* CD003440. Retrieved May 31, 2011, from http://www2.cochrane.org/reviews/en/ab003440.html

Cahill, K., & Perera, R. (2008). Competitions and incentives for smoking cessation. *Cochrane Database of Systematic Reviews, 3,* CD004307. Retrieved May 31, 2011, from http://www2.cochrane.org/reviews/en/ab004307.html

Cahill, K., Stead Lindsay, F., & Lancaster, T. (2008b). Nicotine receptor partial agonists for smoking cessation. *Cochrane Database of Systematic Reviews, 3,* CD006103. Retrieved May 31, 2011, from http://www2.cochrane.org/reviews/en/ab006103.html

Callaghan, R. C., Hathaway, A., Cunningham, J. A., Vettese, L. C., Wyatt, S., Taylor, L., et al. (2005). Does stage-of-change predict dropout in a culturally diverse sample of adolescents admitted to inpatient substance-abuse treatment? A test of the Transtheoretical Model. *Addictive Behaviors, 30* (9), 1834–1847.

Cameron, J., & Ritter, A. (2007). Contingency management: Perspectives of Australian service providers. *Drug & Alcohol Review, 26* (2), 183–189.

Carter, A., Capps, B., & Hall, W. (Eds.). (2009). *Addiction neurobiology: Ethical and social implications.* Luxembourg: Office for Official Publications of the European Communities.

Chikritzhs, T., Fillmore, K., & Stockwell, T. (2009). A healthy dose of scepticism: Four good reasons to think again about protective effects of alcohol on coronary heart disease. *Drug & Alcohol Review, 28* (4), 441–444.

Cicchetti, D., & Rogosch, F. A. (1999). Psychopathology as risk for adolescent substance use disorders: A developmental psychopathology perspective. *Journal of Clinical Child Psychology, 28* (3), 355–365.

Clark N. C., Lintzeris, N., Gijsbers, A., Whelan, G., Dunlop, A., Ritter, A., et al. (2002). LAAM maintenance vs methadone maintenance for heroin dependence. *Cochrane Database of Systematic Reviews, 2,* CD002210. Retrieved June 3, 2011, from http://www2.cochrane.org/reviews/en/ab002210.html

Cleary, M., Hunt, G., Matheson, S., Siegfried, N., & Walter, G. (2008). Psychosocial interventions for people with both severe mental illness and substance misuse. *Cochrane Database of Systematic Reviews, 1,* CD001088. Retrieved June 3, 2011, from http://www2.cochrane.org/reviews/en/ab001088.html

Cloninger, C. R. (1987). A systematic method for clinical description and classification of personality variants. A proposal. *Archives of General Psychiatry, 44* (6), 573–588.

Cohen, E., Feinn, R., Arias, A., & Kranzler, H. R. (2007). Alcohol treatment utilization: Findings from the National Epidemiologic Survey on Alcohol and Related Conditions. *Drug and Alcohol Dependence, 86* (2–3), 214–221.

Collins, D. J., & Lapsley, H. M. (2008a). *The avoidable costs of alcohol abuse in Australia and the potential benefits of effective policies to reduce the social costs of alcohol.* Canberra: Commonwealth Department of Health and Ageing.

Collins, D. J., & Lapsley, H. M. (2008b). The costs of tobacco, alcohol and illicit drug abuse to Australian society in 2004/05. Canberra: Commonwealth of Australia. Retrieved June 3, 2011, from http://www.health.gov.au/internet/drugstrategy/publishing.nsf/Content/34F55AF632F67B70CA2573F60005D42B/$File/mono64.pdf

Compton, W. M., Thomas, Y. F., Stinson, F. S., & Grant, B. F. (2007). Prevalence, correlates, disability, and comorbidity of DSM-IV drug abuse and dependence in the United States: Results from the national epidemiologic survey on alcohol and related conditions. *Archives of General Psychiatry, 64* (5), 566–576.

Conrod, P. J., Castellanos, N., & Strang, J. (2010). Brief, personality-targeted coping skills interventions prolong survival as a non-drug user over a two-year period during adolescence. *Archives of General Psychiatry, 67* (1), 85–93.

Copeland, J., Gilmour, S., Gates, P., & Swift, W. (2005). The Cannabis Problems Questionnaire: Factor structure, reliability, and validity. *Drug & Alcohol Dependence, 80* (3), 313–319.

Copeland, J., & Maxwell, J. C. (2007). Cannabis treatment outcomes among legally coerced and non-coerced adults. *BMC Public Health, 7*, 111.

Copersino, M. L., Boyd, S. J., Tashkin, D. P., Huestis, M. A., Heishman, S. J., Dermand, J. C., et al. (2006). Cannabis withdrawal among non-treatment-seeking adult cannabis users. *American Journal on Addictions, 15* (1), 8–14.

Cornelius, J. R., Chung, T., Martin, C., Wood, D. S., & Clark, D. B. (2008). Cannabis withdrawal is common among treatment-seeking adolescents with cannabis dependence and major depression, and is associated with rapid relapse to dependence. *Addictive Behaviors, 33* (11), 1500–1505.

Cornelius, J. R., Salloum, I. M., Haskett, R. F., Ehler, J. G., Jarrett, P. J., Thase, M. E., et al. (1999). Fluoxetine versus placebo for the marijuana use of depressed alcoholics. *Addictive Behaviors, 24* (1), 111–114.

Costello, E., Erkanli, A., Federman, E., & Angold, A. (1999). Development of psychiatric comorbidity with substance abuse in adolescents: Effects of timing and sex. *Journal of Clinical Child Psychology, 28* (3), 298–311.

Covey, L. S. (1999). Tobacco cessation among patients with depression. *Primary Care, 26* (3), 691–706.

Cubells, J. F., Feinn, R., Pearson, D., Burda, J., Tang, Y., Farrer, L. A., et al. (2005). Rating the severity and character of transient cocaine-induced delusions and hallucinations with a new instrument, the Scale for Assessment of Positive Symptoms for Cocaine-Induced Psychosis (SAPS-CIP). *Drug & Alcohol Dependence, 80* (1), 23–33.

Darke, S., Kaye, S., McKetin, R., & Duflou, J. (2007). *Physical and psychological harms of psychostimulant use.* Sydney: National Drug & Alcohol Research Centre.

Darke, S., Kaye, S., McKetin, R., & Duflou, J. (2008). Major physical and psychological harms of methamphetamine use. *Drug & Alcohol Review, 27* (3), 253–262.

Darke, S., & Ross, J. (1997). Overdose risk perceptions and behaviours among heroin users in Sydney, Australia. *European Addiction Research, 3* (2), 87–92.

Darke, S., Ward, J., Hall, W., Heather, N.,

& Wodak, A. (1991). *The opiate treatment index (OTI) manual* (Technical Report No. 11). Sydney: National Drug and Alcohol Research Centre.

Davies, D. L. (1962). Normal drinking in recovered alcohol addicts. *Quarterly Journal of Studies on Alcohol, 21,* 94–104.

Davis, R. M., Wakefield, M., Amos, A., & Gupta, P. C. (2007). The hitchhiker's guide to tobacco control: A global assessment of harms, remedies, and controversies. *Annual Review of Public Health, 28,* 171–194.

Dawe, S., Loxton, N. J., Hides, L., Kavanagh, D. J., & Mattick, R. P. (2002). *Review of diagnostic and screening for alcohol and other drug use and other psychiatric disorders.* Canberra: Commonwealth Department of Health and Aged Care.

Dawson, D. A., Grant, B. F., & Stinson, F. S. (2005a). The AUDIT-C: Screening for alcohol use disorders and risk drinking in the presence of other psychiatric disorders. *Comprehensive Psychiatry, 46* (6), 405–416.

Dawson, D. A., Grant, B. F., Stinson, F. S., & Zhou, Y. (2005b). Effectiveness of the derived Alcohol Use Disorders Identification Test (AUDIT-C) in screening for alcohol use disorders and risk drinking in the US general population. *Alcoholism: Clinical & Experimental Research, 29* (5), 844–854.

Day, E., Ison, J., & Strang, J. (2005). Inpatient versus other settings for detoxification for opioid dependence. *Cochrane Database of Systematic Reviews,* 2, CD004580. Retrieved June 3, 2011, from http://www2.cochrane.org/reviews/en/ab004580.html

Degenhardt, L., Bruno, R., & Topp, L. (2010a). Is ecstasy a drug of dependence? *Drug and Alcohol Dependence, 107,* 1–10.

Degenhardt, L., Calabria, B., Hall, W., & Lynskey, M. (2008). *Overview of proposed injuries/diseases to be included in the comparative risk assessment for regular cannabis use. Global Burden of Disease Mental Disorders and Illicit Drug Use Expert Group* (Illicit drugs discussion paper No. 5). Sydney: National Drug and Alcohol Research Centre, University of New South Wales.

Degenhardt, L., Coffey, C., Carlin, J. B., Swift, W., Moore, E., & Patton, G. C. (2010b). Outcomes of occasional cannabis use in adolescence: 10-year follow-up study in Victoria, Australia. *British Journal of Psychiatry, 196,* 290–295.

Degenhardt, L., Hall, W., Korten, A., & Jablensky, A. (2005). *Use of brief screening instrument for psychosis: Results of a ROC analysis.* (Technical Report No. 210). Sydney: National Drug and Alcohol Research Centre.

Degenhardt, L., Hall, W., & Lynskey, M. (2001). Alcohol, cannabis and tobacco use among Australians: A comparison of their associations with other drug use and use disorders, affective and anxiety disorders, and psychosis. *Addiction, 96* (11), 1603–1614.

Degenhardt, L., Roxburgh, A., Black, E., & Dunn, M. (2006). *Accidental drug-induced deaths due to opioids in Australia, 2004.* Sydney: National Drug and Alcohol Research Centre.

Degenhardt, L. D., Hall, W. D., Warner-Smith, M., & Lynskey, M. (2004). Illicit drug use. In M. Ezzati, A. D. Lopez, A. Rodgers, & C. J. L. Murray (Eds.), *Comparative quantification of health risks: Global and regional burden of disease attributable to selected major risk factors* (Vol. 1, pp. 1109–1176). Geneva: World Health Organization.

Denis, C., Lavie, E., Fatseas, M., & Auriacombe, M. (2006). Psychotherapeutic interventions for cannabis abuse and/or dependence in outpatient settings. *Cochrane Database of Systematic Reviews,* 3, CD005336. Retrieved June 3, 2011, from http://

www2.cochrane.org/reviews/en/ab005336.html

Di Chiara, G., & North, R. A. (1992). Neurobiology of opiate abuse. *Trends in Pharmacological Science, 13,* 185–193.

Diaz, R., & Fruhauf, A. (1991). The origins and development of self-regulation: A developmental model on the risk for addictive behaviours. In N. Heather, W. Miller, & J. Greeley (Eds.), *Self-control and the addictive behaviours* (pp. 83–106). Sydney: Maxwell Macmillan Publishing Australia.

Dole, V. P., & Nyswander, M. (1965). A medical treatment for diacetylmorphine (heroin) addiction. *JAMA, 193,* 80–84.

Drews, E., & Zimmer, A. (2010). Modulation of alcohol and nicotine responses through the endogenous opioid system. *Progress in Neurobiology, 90* (1), 1–15.

Druginfo Clearinghouse: The Drug Prevention Network. (2010). *Effects of amphetamines.* Sydney: Australian Drug Foundation. Retrieved June 3, 2011, from http://www.druginfo.adf.org.au/hidden_articles/amphetamines.html#effects

Drummond, C., Coulton, S., James, D., Godfrey, C., Parrott, S., Baxter, J., et al. (2009). Effectiveness and cost-effectiveness of a stepped care intervention for alcohol use disorders in primary care: Pilot study. *British Journal of Psychiatry, 195* (5), 448–456.

Drummond, D. C., & Glautier, S. (1994). A controlled trial of cue exposure treatment in alcohol dependence. *Journal of Consulting & Clinical Psychology, 62* (4), 809–817.

Drummond, D. C., Tiffany, S., Glautier, S., & Remington, B. (1995). Cue exposure in understanding and treating addictive behaviours. In D. C. Drummond, S. Tiffany, S. Glautier, & B. Remington (Eds.), *Addictive behaviour: Cue exposure theory and practice* (pp. 1–17). Chichester: John Wiley & Sons Ltd.

Edwards, G., Anderson, P., Babor, T., Casswell, S., Ferrence, R., Giesbrecht, N., et al. (1994). *Alcohol policy and the public good.* Oxford: Oxford University Press.

Edwards, G., Arif, A., & Hodgson, R. (1981). Nomenclature and classification of drug and alcohol related problems: A WHO memorandum. *Bulletin of the World Health Organization, 50,* 225–242.

Edwards, G., & Gross, M. (1976). Alcohol dependence: Provisional description of a clinical syndrome. *British Medical Journal, 1,* 1058–1061.

Edwards, G., Gross, M., Keller, M., Moser, J., & Room, R. (1977). *Alcohol related disabilities* (Offset Publication No. 32). Geneva: World Health Organization.

Elliott, J. C., Carey, K. B., & Bolles, J. R. (2008). Computer-based interventions for college drinking: A qualitative review. *Addictive Behaviors, 33* (8), 994–1005.

Emmen, M. J., Schippers, G. M., Bleijenberg, G., & Wollersheim, H. (2004). Effectiveness of opportunistic brief interventions for problem drinking in a general hospital setting: Systematic review. *BMJ, 328* (7435), 318.

European Commission, Trimbos Institute, & RAND Europe. (2009). *A report on global illicit drugs markets 1998–2007.* Netherlands: European Commission, Directorate-General.

Eysenck, H. (1997). Addiction, personality and motivation. *Human Psychopharmacology, 12,* s79–s87.

Eyseneck, H. J., & Eyseneck, M. W. (1985). *Personality and individual differences.* New York: Plenum Press.

Faggiano, F., Vigna-Taglianti, F. D., Versino, E., Zambon, A., Borraccino, A., & Lemma, P. (2008). School-based prevention for illicit drugs use: A systematic review. *Preventive Medicine, 46* (5), 385–396.

Fergusson, D. M., & Horwood, L. J. (1997).

Early onset cannabis use and psychosocial adjustment in young adults. *Addiction, 92* (3), 279–296.

Ferri, M., Amato, L., & Davoli, M. (2006). Alcoholics Anonymous and other 12-step programmes for alcohol dependence. *Cochrane Database of Systematic Reviews, 3*, CD005032. Retrieved June 3, 2011, from http://www2.cochrane.org/reviews/en/ab005032.html

Ferri, M., Davoli, M., & Perucci Carlo, A. (2010). Heroin maintenance for chronic heroin dependents. *Cochrane Database of Systematic Reviews, 8*, CD003410. Retrieved June 3, 2011, from http://www2.cochrane.org/reviews/en/ab003410.html

Fiore, M. C., Jaen, C. R., Baker, T. B., Bailey, W. C., Benowitz, N. L., Curry, S. J., et al. (2008). *Treating tobacco use and dependence: 2008 update.* Clinical practice Guideline. Rockville, MD: US Department of Health and Human Services, Public Health Service.

Flaherty, B., Homel, P., & Hall, W. (1991). Public attitudes towards alcohol control policies. *Australian Journal of Public Health, 15* (4), 301–306.

Ford, J. D., Gelernter, J., DeVoe, J. S., Zhang, W., Weiss, R. D., Brady, K., et al. (2009). Association of psychiatric and substance use disorder comorbidity with cocaine dependence severity and treatment utilization in cocaine-dependent individuals. *Drug & Alcohol Dependence, 99* (1–3), 193–203.

Foxcroft, D., Ireland, D., Lowe, G., & Breen, R. (2002). Primary prevention for alcohol misuse in young people. *Cochrane Database of Systematic Reviews, 3*, CD003024. Retrieved June 3, 2011, from http://www2.cochrane.org/reviews/en/ab003024.html.

Frank, D., DeBenedetti, A. F., Volk, R. J., Williams, E. C., Kivlahan, D. R., & Bradley, K. A. (2008). Effectiveness of the AUDIT-C as a screening test for alcohol misuse in three race/ethnic groups. *Journal of General Internal Medicine, 23* (6), 781–787.

Garbutt, J. C. (2009). The state of pharmacotherapy for the treatment of alcohol dependence. *Journal of Substance Abuse Treatment, 36* (1), S15–23; quiz S24–15.

Gardner, E. L. (1992). Cannabinoid interaction with brain reward systems – The neurobiological basis of cannabinoid abuse. In L. Murphy, & A. Bartke (Eds.), *Marijuana/cannabinoids: Neurobiology and neurophysiology.* London: CRC Press.

Gartner, C. E., Hall, W. D., Vos, T., Bertram, M. Y., Wallace, A. L., & Lim, S. S. (2007). Assessment of Swedish snus for tobacco harm reduction: An epidemiological modelling study. *Lancet, 369* (9578), 2010–2014.

Geller, B., Cooper, T. B., Sun, K., Zimerman, B., Frazier, J., Williams, M., et al. (1998). Double-blind and placebo-controlled study of lithium for adolescent bipolar disorders with secondary substance dependency. *Journal of the American Academy of Child & Adolescent Psychiatry, 37* (2), 171–178.

Gerra, G., Maremmani, I., Capovani, B., Somaini, L., Berterame, S., Tomas-Rossello, J., et al. (2009). Long-acting opioid-agonists in the treatment of heroin addiction: Why should we call them "substitution"? *Substance Use & Misuse, 44* (5), 663–671.

Gerstein, D. R., & Harwood, H. (1990). *Treating drug problems: A study of effectiveness and financing of public and private drug treatment systems* (Vol. 1). Washington: National Academy Press.

Gittelman, R., Mannuzza, S., Shenker, R., & Bonagura, N. (1985). Hyperactive boys almost grown up: I. Psychiatric status. *Archives of General Psychiatry, 42,* 937–947.

Gmel, G., & Rehm, J. (2003). Harmful alcohol use. *Alcohol Research & Health:*

the *Journal of the National Institute on Alcohol Abuse & Alcoholism, 27* (1), 52–62.

Gold, M. S., Dackis, C. A., & Washton, A. M. (1984). The sequential use of clonidine and naltrexone in the treatment of opiate addicts. *Advances in Alcohol and Substance Abuse, 3* (3), 19–39.

Gomez, A., Conde, A., Santana, J. M., Jorrin, A., Serrano, I. M., & Medina, R. (2006). The diagnostic usefulness of AUDIT and AUDIT-C for detecting hazardous drinkers in the elderly. *Aging & Mental Health, 10* (5), 558–561.

Goodman, A. (2008). Neurobiology of addiction. An integrative review. *Biochemical Pharmacology, 75* (1), 266–322.

Gorman, D. M., & Charles Huber, J., Jr. (2007). Do medical cannabis laws encourage cannabis use? *International Journal of Drug Policy, 18* (3), 160–167.

Gossop, M., Darke, S., Griffiths, P., Hando, J., Powis, B., Hall, W., et al. (1995). The Severity of Dependence Scale (SDS): Psychometric properties of the SDS in English and Australian samples of heroin, cocaine and amphetamine users. *Addiction, 90,* 607–614.

Gourlay, S. G., Stead, L. F., & Benowitz, N. (2004). Clonidine for smoking cessation. *Cochrane Database of Systematic Reviews,* 3, CD000058. Retrieved May 31, 2011, from http://www2.cochrane.org/ reviews/en/ab000058.html

Gowing, L. R., Ali, R. L., & White, J. M. (2000). *Respiratory harms of smoked cannabis* (Monograph No. 8). Adelaide: Drug and Alcohol Services Council.

Gowing, L., Ali, R., & White J. M. (2009a). Buprenorphine for the management of opioid withdrawal. *Cochrane Database of Systematic Reviews,* 3, CD002025. Retrieved May 31, 2011, from http:// www2.cochrane.org/reviews/en/ ab002025.html

Gowing, L., Ali, R., & White, J. M. (2009b). Opioid antagonists with minimal sedation for opioid withdrawal. *Cochrane Database of Systematic Reviews,* 4, CD002021. Retrieved May 31, 2011, from http://www2.cochrane.org/ reviews/en/ab002021.html

Gowing, L., Ali, R., & White, J. M. (2010). Opioid antagonists under heavy sedation or anaesthesia for opioid withdrawal. *Cochrane Database of Systematic Reviews,* 1, CD002022. Retrieved May 31, 2011, from http:// www2.cochrane.org/reviews/en/ ab002022.html

Gowing, L., Farrell, M., Ali, R., & White, J. M. (2009c). Alpha2-adrenergic agonists for the management of opioid withdrawal. *Cochrane Database of Systematic Reviews,* 2, CD002024. Retrieved May 31, 2011, from http:// www2.cochrane.org/reviews/en/ ab002024.html

Grant, B. F., Hasin, D. S., Chou, S. P., Stinson, F. S., & Dawson, D. A. (2004a). Nicotine dependence and psychiatric disorders in the United States: Results from the national epidemiologic survey on alcohol and related conditions. *Archives of General Psychiatry, 61* (11), 1107–1115.

Grant, B. F., Stinson, F. S., Dawson, D. A., Chou, S. P., Dufour, M. C., Compton, W., et al. (2004b). Prevalence and co-occurrence of substance use disorders and independent mood and anxiety disorders: Results from the National Epidemiologic Survey on Alcohol and Related Conditions. *Archives of General Psychiatry, 61* (8), 807–816.

Greeley, J., Swift, W., & Heather, N. (1992). Depressed affect as a predictor of increased desire for alcohol in current drinkers of alcohol. *British Journal of Addiction, 87* (7), 1005–1012.

Hajek, P., & Stead, L. F. (2001). Aversive smoking for smoking cessation. *Cochrane Database of Systematic Reviews,* 3, CD000546. Retrieved May 31, 2011, from http://www2.cochrane.org/reviews/en/ab000546.html

Halikas, J. A., Crosby, R. D., & Nugent, S. M. (1992). The convergent validity of the Drug Impairment Rating Scale for cocaine. *Psychopharmacology Bulletin, 28,* (3), 315–318.

Halikas, J. A., Nugent, S. M., Crosby, R. D., & Carlson, G. A. (1993). 1990–1991 survey of pharmacotherapies used in the treatment of cocaine abuse. *Journal of Addictive Diseases, 12,* (2), 129–139.

Hall, W. (1997). Addiction. Highs and lows. *Lancet, 350* (Suppl. 3), SIII1.

Hall, W. (2002). The prospects for immunotherapy in smoking cessation. *Lancet, 360* (9339), 1089–1091.

Hall, W. (2009). The adverse health effects of cannabis use: What are they, and what are their implications for policy? *International Journal of Drug Policy, 20* (6), 458–466.

Hall, W., & Degenhardt, L. (2009). Adverse health effects of non-medical cannabis use. *Lancet, 374* (9698), 1383–1391.

Hall, W., Degenhardt, L., & Lynskey, M. (2001). *The health and psychological effects of cannabis use* (2nd ed.). Canberra: Australian Government Department of Health and Ageing.

Hall, W., Degenhardt, L., & Teesson, M. (2009). Understanding and responding to comorbidity: The need to broaden the research base? *Addictive Behaviours, 34,* 526–530.

Hall, W., & Gartner, C. (2009). Supping with the devil? The role of law in promoting tobacco harm reduction using low nitrosamine smokeless tobacco products. *Public Health, 123* (3), 287–291.

Hall, W., Johnston, L., & Donnelly, N. (1999a). Epidemiology of cannabis use and its consequences. In H. Kalant, W. Corrigall, W. Hall, & R. Smart (Eds.), *The health effects of cannabis* (pp. 71–125). Toronto, Canada: Centre for Addiction and Mental Health.

Hall, W., Teesson, M., Lynskey, M., & Degenhardt, L. (1999b). The 12-month prevalence of substance use and ICD-10 substance use disorders in Australian adults: Findings from the National Survey of Mental Health and Well-Being. *Addiction, 94* (10), 1541–1550.

Hall, W. D., & Mattick, R. P. (2007). Clinical update: Codeine maintenance in opioid dependence. *Lancet, 370* (9587), 550–552.

Hasin, D. S., Stinson, F. S., Ogburn, E., & Grant, B. F. (2007). Prevalence, correlates, disability, and comorbidity of DSM-IV alcohol abuse and dependence in the United States: Results from the National Epidemiologic Survey on Alcohol and Related Conditions. *Archives of General Psychiatry, 64* (7), 830–842.

Hathaway, A. D., Callaghan, R. C., Macdonald, S., & Erickson, P. G. (2009). Cannabis dependence as a primary drug use-related problem: The case for harm reduction-oriented treatment options. *Substance Use & Misuse, 44* (7), 990–1008.

Hawkins, J., Catalano, R., & Miller, J. (1992). Risk and protective factors for alcohol and other drug problems in adolescence and early adulthood: Implications for substance abuse prevention. *Psychological Bulletin, 112,* 64–105.

Hayashida, M., Alterman, A. I., McLellan, A. T., O'Brien, C. P., Purtill, J. J., Volpicelli, J. R., et al. (1989). Comparative effectiveness and costs of inpatient and outpatient detoxification of patients with mild-to-moderate alcohol withdrawal syndrome. *The New England Journal of Medicine, 320,* 358–365.

Hayes, L., Smart, D., Toumbourou, J. W., & Sanson, A. (2004). *Parenting influences on adolescent alcohol use* (Research Report No. 10). Melbourne: Australian Institute

of Family Studies, Commonwealth of
Australia.

Hays, J. T., Ebbert, J. O., & Sood, A. (2009).
Treating tobacco dependence in light of
the 2008 US Department of Health and
Human Services clinical practice
guideline. *Mayo Clinic Proceedings, 84*
(8), 730–735; quiz 735–736.

Heath, D. B. (2000). *Drinking occasions:
Comparative perspectives on alcohol and
culture.* Ann Arbor, MI: Sheridan Books.

Heather, M. (Ed.). (1998). *Using brief
opportunities for change in medical settings*
(2nd ed.). New York: Plenum Press.

Heather, N., & Greeley, J. (1990). Cue
exposure in the treatment of drug
dependence: The potential of a new
method for preventing relapse. *Drug
and Alcohol Review, 9,* 155–168.

Heather, N., & Robertson, I. (1993).
Controlled drinking. London: Methuen.

Heather, N., & Tebbutt, J. (1989). *The
effectiveness of treatment for drug and
alcohol problems: An overview.* Canberra:
Commonwealth Department of
Community Services and Health:
National Campaign Against Drug
Abuse (NCADA).

Heatherton, T., Kozlowski, L., Frecker, R.,
& Fagerström, K. (1991). The
Fagerström Test for Nicotine
Dependence: A revision of the
Fagerström Tolerance Questionnaire.
British Journal of Addiction, 86,
1119–1127.

Helzer, J., Burnam, A., & McEvoy, L.
(1991). Alcohol abuse and dependence.
In L. N. Robins, & D. A. Regier (Eds.),
Psychiatric disorders in America (pp.
81–115). New York: The Free Press.

Heng, K., Hargarten, S., Layde, P., Craven,
A., & Zhu, S. (2006). Moderate alcohol
intake and motor vehicle crashes: The
conflict between health advantage and
at-risk use. *Alcohol & Alcoholism, 41* (4),
451–454.

Herrnstein, R., & Prelec, D. (1992). A
theory of addiction. In G. Loewenstein,

& J. Elster (Eds.), *Choice over time.* New
York: The Russell Sage Foundation.

Hesse, M. (2006). The Readiness Ruler as a
measure of readiness to change polydrug use in drug abusers. *Harm
Reduction Journal, 3* (3). Retrieved June
3, 2011, from http://
www.ncbi.nlm.nih.gov/pmc/articles/
PMC1395301/

Hingson, R., & Winter, M. (2003).
Epidemiology and consequences of
drinking and driving. *Alcohol Research
& Health: the Journal of the National
Institute on Alcohol Abuse & Alcoholism,
27* (1), 63–78.

Hofler, M., Lieb, R., Perkonigg, A.,
Schuster, P., Sonntag, H., & Wittchen,
H.-U. (1999). Covariates of cannabis use
progression in a representative
population sample of adolescents: A
prospective examination of
vulnerability and risk factors. *Addiction,
94* (11), 1679–1694.

Homel, R. (1989). Crime on the roads:
Drinking and driving. In J. Vernon
(Ed.), *Alcohol and crime.* Canberra:
Australian Institute of Criminology.

Hoogendoorn, M., Welsing, P., & Rutten-
van Molken, M. P. M. H. (2008). Cost-
effectiveness of varenicline compared
with bupropion, NRT, and nortriptyline
for smoking cessation in the
Netherlands. *Current Medical Research &
Opinion, 24* (1), 51–61.

Hubbard, R. L., Craddock, S. G., Flynn, P.
M., Anderson, J., & Etheridge, R. M.
(1997). Overview of 1-year follow-up
outcomes in the Drug Abuse Treatment
Outcome Study (DATOS). *Psychology of
Addictive Behaviors, 11* (4), 261–278.

Hughes, J. R., Stead, L. F., & Lancaster, T.
(2000). Anxioloytics and
antidepressants for smoking cessation.
The Cochrane Library, Issue 3. Oxford:
Update Software.

Hughes, J. R., Stead, L. F., & Lancaster, T.
(2007). Antidepressants for smoking
cessation. *Cochrane Database of*

Systematic Reviews, 1, CD000031. Retrieved June 3, 2011, from http://www2.cochrane.org/reviews/en/ab000031.html

Hulse, G. K., English, D. R., Milne, E., & Holman, C. D. (1999). The quantification of mortality resulting from the regular use of illicit opiates. *Addiction*, 94 (2), 221–229.

Hulse, G. K., Morris, N., Arnold-Reed, D., & Tait, R. J. (2009). Improving clinical outcomes in treating heroin dependence: Randomized, controlled trial of oral or implant naltrexone. *Archives of General Psychiatry*, 66 (10), 1108–1115.

Institute of Medicine. (1996). *Pathways of addiction*. Washington, DC: National Academy Press.

International Center for Alcohol Policies. (2010). *International Drinking Guidelines*. Washington, DC: ICAP. Retrieved June 3, 2011, from http://www.icap.org/

Jarvis, T. J., Tebbutt, J., Mattick, R. P., & Shand, F. (2005). *Treatment approaches for alcohol and drug dependence – An introductory guide* (2nd ed.). Chichester: Wiley.

Johnsson, K. O., & Berglund, M. (2006). Comparison between a cognitive behavioural alcohol programme and post-mailed minimal intervention in high-risk drinking university freshmen: Results from a randomized controlled trial. *Alcohol & Alcoholism*, 41 (2), 174–180.

Kampman, K. M., Volpicelli, J. R., McGinnis, D. E., Alterman, A. I., Weinreib, R. M., D'Angelo, L., et al. (1998). Reliability and validity of the Cocaine Selective Severity Assessment. *Addictive Behaviors*, 23, (4), 449–461.

Kaner, E. F. S., Dickinson, H. O., Beyer, F. R., Campbell, F., Schlesinger, C., Heather, N., et al. (2007). Effectiveness of brief alcohol interventions in primary care populations. *Cochrane Database of Systematic Reviews*, 3, CD004148.

Kaysen, D., Dillworth, T. M., Simpson, T., Waldrop, A., Larimer, M. E., & Resick, P. A. (2007). Domestic violence and alcohol use: Trauma-related symptoms and motives for drinking. *Addictive Behaviors*, 32 (6), 1272–1283.

Kendler, K. S., Davis, C. G., & Kessler, R. C. (1997). The familial aggregation of common psychiatric and substance use disorders in the National Comorbidity Survey: A family history study. *British Journal of Psychiatry*, 170, 541–548.

Kendler, K. S., Jacobson, K. C., Prescott, C. A., & Neale, M. C. (2003). Specificity of genetic and environmental risk factors for use and abuse/dependence of cannabis, cocaine, hallucinogens, sedatives, stimulants, and opiates in male twins. *American Journal of Psychiatry*, 160 (4), 687–695.

Kendler, K. S., Myers, J., & Prescott, C. A. (2007). Specificity of genetic and environmental risk factors for symptoms of cannabis, cocaine, alcohol, caffeine, and nicotine dependence. *Archives of General Psychiatry*, 64 (11), 1313–1320.

Kessler, R. C. (1996). *Kessler's 10 Psychological Distress Scale*. Boston, MA: Harvard Medical School.

Kessler, R. C., Chiu, W. T., Demler, O., Merikangas, K. R., & Walters, E. E. (2005). Prevalence, severity, and comorbidity of 12-month DSM-IV disorders in the National Comorbidity Survey Replication. *Archives of General Psychiatry*, 62 (6), 617–627.

Kessler, R. C., McGonagh, K. A., Zhao, S., Nelson, C. B., Hughes, M., Eshleman, S., et al. (1994). Lifetime and 12-month prevalence of DSM-III-R psychiatric disorders in the United States. *Archives of General Psychiatry*, 51, 8–19.

Kleber, H. D. (1998). Ultrarapid opiate detoxifications. *Addiction*, 93 (11), 1629–1633.

Knapp, W. P., Soares, B., Farrell, M., & Silva de Lima, M. (2007). Psychosocial interventions for cocaine and psychostimulant amphetamines related disorders. *Cochrane Database of Systematic Reviews, 3,* CD003023.

Koob, G., & Le Moal, M. (1997). Drug abuse: Hedonic homeostatic dysregulation. *Lancet, 278,* 52–58.

Koob, G. E., & Le Moal, M. (2008). Addiction and the brain antireward system. *Annual Review of Psychology, 59,* 29–53.

Kosten, T. (1990). Current pharmacotherapies for opiate dependence. *Psychopharmacology Bulletin, 26,* 69–74.

Krishnan-Sarin, S., Rosen, M., & O'Malley, S. (1999). Preliminary evidence of an opioid component in nicotine dependence. *Archives of General Psychiatry, 56,* 663–668.

Kunoe, N., Lobmaier, P., Vederhus, J. K., Hjerkinn, B., Hegstad, S., Gossop, M., et al. (2009). Naltrexone implants after in-patient treatment for opioid dependence: Randomised controlled trial. *British Journal of Psychiatry, 194* (6), 541–546.

Lancaster, T., & Stead, L. F. (2005a). Individual behavioural counselling for smoking cessation. *Cochrane Database of Systematic Reviews, 2,* CD001292. Retrieved June 3, 2011, from http://www2.cochrane.org/reviews/en/ab001292.html

Lancaster, T., & Stead, L. F. (2005b). Self-help interventions for smoking cessation. *Cochrane Database of Systematic Reviews, 3,* CD001118. Retrieved June 3, 2011, from http://www2.cochrane.org/reviews/en/ab001118.html

Laslett, A.-M., Catalano, P., Chikritzhs, Y., Dale, C., Doran, C., Ferris, J., et al. (2010). *The range and magnitude of alcohol's harm to others.* Melbourne: AER Centre for Alcohol Policy Research, Turning Point Alcohol and Drug Centre, Eastern Health.

Le Merrer, J., Becker, J. A. J., Befort, K., & Kieffer, B. L. (2009). Reward processing by the opioid system in the brain. *Physiological Reviews, 89* (4), 1379–1412.

Lenroot, R. K., & Giedd, J. N. (2006). Brain development in children and adolescents: Insights from anatomical magnetic resonance imaging. *Neuroscience & Biobehavioral Reviews, 30* (6), 718–729.

Leone, M. A., Vigna-Taglianti, F., Avanzi, G., Brambilla, R., & Faggiano, F. (2010). Gamma-hydroxybutyrate (GHB) for treatment of alcohol withdrawal and prevention of relapses. *Cochrane Database of Systematic Reviews, 2,* CD006266. Retrieved June 3, 2011, from http://www2.cochrane.org/reviews/en/ab006266.html

Ling, W., & Wesson, D. R. (1984). Naltrexone treatment for addicted health-care professionals: A collaborative private practice experience. *Journal of Clinical Psychiatry, 45,* 46–48.

Lobmaier, P., Kornor, H., Kunoe, N., & Bjørndal, A. (2008). Sustained-release naltrexone for opioid dependence. *Cochrane Database of Systematic Reviews, 2,* CD006140. Retrieved June 3, 2011, from http://www2.cochrane.org/reviews/en/ab006140.html

Loeber, R., Southamer-Lober, M., & White, H. (1999). Developmental aspects of delinquency and internalising problems and their association with persistent juvenile substance use between ages 7 and 18. *Journal of Clinical Child Psychology, 28,* 322–332.

Loeber, S., Croissant, B., Heinz, A., Mann, K., & Flor, H. (2006). Cue exposure in the treatment of alcohol dependence: effects on drinking outcome, craving and self-efficacy. *British Journal of Clinical Psychology, 45* (4), 515–529.

Lopez, A. D., Mathers, C. D., Ezzati, M.,

Jamison, D. T., & Murray, C. J. L. (2006). *Global burden of disease and risk factors.* Washington, DC: World Bank and New York: Oxford University Press. Retrieved June 3, 2011, from http://files.dcp2.org/pdf/GBD/GBD.pdf

Lovibond, S. H., & Lovibond, P. F. (1995). *Manual for the Depression Anxiety Stress Scales* (2nd ed.). Sydney: Psychology Foundation.

Lubman, D. I., Yucel, M., & Hall, W. D. (2007). Substance use and the adolescent brain: A toxic combination? *Journal of Psychopharmacology, 21* (8), 792–794.

Lynskey, M., & Hall, W. (1998). *Cannabis use among Australian youth* (NDARC Technical Report No. 66). Sydney: National Drug and Alcohol Research Centre.

Madden, P. A. F., Bucholz, K. K., Dinwiddie, S. H., Slutske, W. S., Bierut, L. J., Statham, D. J., et al. (1997). Nicotine withdrawal in women. *Addiction, 92* (7), 889–902.

Magill, M., & Ray, L. A. (2009). Cognitive-behavioral treatment with adult alcohol and illicit drug users: A meta-analysis of randomized controlled trials. *Journal of Studies on Alcohol & Drugs, 70* (4), 516–527.

Maisto, S. A., Clifford, P. R., Stout, R. L., & Davis, C. M. (2007). Moderate drinking in the first year after treatment as a predictor of three-year outcomes. [Erratum appears in *Journal of Studies on Alcohol & Drugs*, 2008, 69 (4), 622]. *Journal of Studies on Alcohol & Drugs, 68* (3), 419–427.

Mak, A. S., & Kinsella, C. (1996). Adolescent drinking, conduct problems, and parental bonding. *Australian Journal of Psychology, 48* (1), 15–20.

Markou, A. (2008). Review. Neurobiology of nicotine dependence. *Philosophical Transactions of the Royal Society of London – Series B: Biological Sciences, 363* (1507), 3159–3168.

Marlatt, G. A., & Donovan, D. M. (Eds.). (2005). *Relapse prevention: Maintenance strategies in the treatment of addictive behaviors* (2nd ed.). New York: Guilford.

Marlatt, G. A., & VandenBos, G. R. (1997). *Addictive behaviors: Readings on etiology, prevention, and treatment.* Washington, DC: American Psychological Association.

Mattick, R. P., & Baillie, A. (1992). *An outline for approaches to smoking cessation: Quality assurance in the treatment of a drug dependence project.* Canberra: Australian Government Publishing Service.

Mattick, R. P., Breen, C., Kimber, J., & Davoli, M. (2009). Methadone maintenance therapy versus no opioid replacement therapy for opioid dependence. *Cochrane Database of Systematic Reviews, 3,* CD002209. Retrieved June 3, 2011, from http://www2.cochrane.org/reviews/en/ab002209.html

Mattick, R. P., & Hall, W. (1993). *A treatment outline for approaches to opioid dependence.* Sydney: National Drug and Alcohol Research Centre (NDARC).

Mattick, R. P., & Hall, W. (1996). Are detoxification programs effective? *Lancet, 347* (1), 97–100.

Mattick, R. P., & Jarvis, T. (Eds.). (1993). *An outline for the management of alcohol problems: Quality assurance project.* Canberra: Australian Government Publishing Service.

Mattick, R. P., Kimber, J., Breen, C., & Davoli, M. (2008). Buprenorphine maintenance versus placebo or methadone maintenance for opioid dependence. *Cochrane Database of Systematic Reviews, 2,* CD002207. Retrieved June 3, 2011, from http://www2.cochrane.org/reviews/en/ab002207.html

Maurer, P., & Bachmann, M. F. (2007).

Vaccination against nicotine: An emerging therapy for tobacco dependence. *Expert Opinion on Investigational Drugs, 16* (11), 1775–1783.

May, P. A., & Gossage, J. P. (2001). Estimating the prevalence of fetal alcohol syndrome. A summary. *Alcohol Research & Health: the Journal of the National Institute on Alcohol Abuse & Alcoholism, 25* (3), 159–167.

Mayet, S., Farrell, M., Ferri, M., Amato, L., & Davoli, M. (2004). Psychosocial treatment for opiate abuse and dependence. *Cochrane Database of Systematic Reviews, 4*, CD004330. Retrieved June 3, 2011, from http://www2.cochrane.org/reviews/en/ab004330.html

McClure, J. B. (2001). Are biomarkers a useful aid in smoking cessation? A review and analysis of the literature. *Behavioral Medicine, 27* (1), 37–47.

McCrady, B. S., Epstein, E. E., Cook, S., Jensen, N., & Hildebrandt, T. (2009). A randomized trial of individual and couple behavioral alcohol treatment for women. *Journal of Consulting & Clinical Psychology, 77* (2), 243–256.

McGregor, C., Srisurapanont, M., Mitchell, A., Longo, M. C., Cahill, S., & White, J. M. (2008). Psychometric evaluation of the Amphetamine Cessation Symptom Assessment. *Journal of Substance Abuse Treatment, 34* (4), 443–449.

McLaren, J., & Mattick, R. (2007). *Monograph Series No 57: Cannabis in Australia – Use, supply, harms and responses*. Canberra: National Drug Strategy, Department of Health and Ageing.

McLellan, A. T., Kushner, H., Metzger, D., Peters, R., Smith, I., Grissom, G., et al. (1992). The Fifth Edition of the Addiction Severity Index. *Journal of Substance Abuse Treatment, 9* (3), 199–213.

McLellan A. T., Woody, G. E., Metzger, D., McKay, J., Durell, J., Alterman, A., et al.

(1997). Evaluating the effectiveness of addiction treatment: Reasonable expectations, appropriate comparisons. In J. A. Egertson, D. M. Fox, & A. I. Leshner (Eds.), *Treating drug abusers effectively*. Malden, MA: Blackwell and Milbank Memorial Fund.

McQueen, J., Howe, T. E., Allan, L., & Mains, D. (2009). Brief interventions for heavy alcohol users admitted to general hospital wards. *Cochrane Database of Systematic Reviews, 3*, CD005191.

Merikangas, K. R., Stevens, D. E., Fenton, B., Stolar, M., O'Malley, S., Woods, S. W., et al. (1998). Co-morbidity and familial aggregation of alcoholism and anxiety disorders. *Psychological Medicine, 28* (4), 773–788.

Mewton, L., Slade, T., McBride, O., Grove, R., & Teesson, M. (2011). An evaluation of the proposed DSM-5 alcohol use disorder criteria using Australian national data. *Addiction, 106* (5), 941–950.

Miller, W., & Brown, J. (1991). Self-regulation as a conceptual basis for the prevention and treatment of addictive behaviours. In N. Heather, W. Miller, & J. Greeley (Eds.), *Self-control and the addictive behaviours*. Sydney: Maxwell Macmillan Publishing Australia.

Miller, W., & Rollnick, S. (1991). *Motivational interviewing: Preparing people to change addictive behaviour*. New York: Guilford.

Miller, W. R. (1980). The addictive behaviors. In W. R. Miller (Ed.), *The addictive behaviors* (pp. 3–7). Oxford: Pergamon Press.

Miller, W. R., & Marlatt, G. A. (1984). *Comprehensive Drinker Profile (CDP)*. Odessa, FL: Psychological Assessment Resources.

Miller, W. R., & Rollnick, S. (2002). *Motivational interviewing: Preparing people to change addictive behaviour* (2nd ed.). New York: Guilford Press.

Miller, W. R., & Tonigan, J. S. (1996).

Assessing drinkers' motivations for change: The Stages of Change Readiness and Treatment Eagerness Scale (SOCRATES). *Psychology of Addictive Behaviors, 10* (2), 81–89.

Miller, W. R., Walters, S. T., & Bennett, M. E. (2001). How effective is alcoholism treatment in the United States? *Journal of Studies on Alcohol, 62* (2), 211–220.

Miller, W. R., & Wilbourne, P. L. (2002). Mesa Grande: A methodological analysis of clinical trials of treatment for alcohol use disorders. *Addiction, 97* (3), 265–277.

Mills, K., Deady, M., Proudfoot, H., Sannibale, C., Teesson, M., Mattick, R., et al. (2009). *Guidelines on the management of co-occurring alcohol and other drug and mental health conditions in alcohol and other drug treatment settings.* Sydney: National Drug and Alcohol Research Centre.

Mills, K. L., Lynskey, M., Teesson, M., Ross, J., & Darke, S. (2005a). Post-traumatic stress disorder among people with heroin dependence in the Australian treatment outcome study (ATOS): Prevalence and correlates. *Drug & Alcohol Dependence, 77* (3), 243–249.

Mills, K. L., Teesson, M., Ross, J., Darke, S., & Shanahan, M. (2005b). The costs and outcomes of treatment for opioid dependence associated with posttraumatic stress disorder. *Psychiatric Services, 56* (8), 940–945.

Mills, K. L., Teesson, M., Ross, J., & Peters, L. (2006). Trauma, PTSD, and substance use disorders: findings from the Australian National Survey of Mental Health and Well-Being. *American Journal of Psychiatry, 163* (4), 652–658.

Minozzi, S., Amato, L., Davoli, M., Farrell, M., Lima Reisser, A. A. R. L., Pani, P. P., et al. (2008). Anticonvulsants for cocaine dependence. *Cochrane Database of Systematic Reviews, 2*, CD006754. Retrieved June 3, 2011, from http:// www2.cochrane.org/reviews/en/ ab006754.html

Minozzi, S., Amato, L., Vecchi, S., & Davoli, M. (2010). Anticonvulsants for alcohol withdrawal. *Cochrane Database of Systematic Reviews, 3*, CD005064. Retrieved June 3, 2011, from http:// www2.cochrane.org/reviews/en/ ab005064.html

Minozzi, S., Amato, L., Vecchi, S., Davoli, M., Kirchmayer, U., & Verster, A. (2011). Oral naltrexone maintenance treatment for opioid dependence. *Cochrane Database of Systematic Reviews, 4*, CD001333. Retrieved June 3, 2011, from http://www2.cochrane.org/ reviews/en/ab001333.html

Mohapatra, S., Patra, J., Popova, S., Duhig, A., & Rehm, J. (2010). Social cost of heavy drinking and alcohol dependence in high-income countries. *International Journal of Public Health, 55* (3), 149–157.

Monti, P. M., & Rohsenow, D. J. (1999). Coping-skills training and cue-exposure therapy in the treatment of alcoholism. *Alcohol Research & Health: The Journal of the National Institute on Alcohol Abuse & Alcoholism, 23* (2), 107–115.

Moreira, M. T., Smith, L. A., & Foxcroft, D. (2009). Social norms interventions to reduce alcohol misuse in University or College students. *Cochrane Database of Systematic Reviews, 3*, CD006748.

Morley, K. C., Teesson, M., Reid, S. C., Sannibale, C., Thomson, C., Phung, N., et al. (2006). Naltrexone versus acamprosate in the treatment of alcohol dependence: A multi-centre, randomized, double-blind, placebo-controlled trial. *Addiction, 101* (10), 1451–1462.

Murtagh, J., & Foerster, V. (2007). Nicotine vaccines for smoking cessation. *Issues in Emerging Health Technologies, 103*, 1–4.

National Institute on Alcohol Abuse and Alcoholism and National Institutes of

Health. (2005). *Helping patients who drink too much: A clinician's guide* (Updated 2005 ed.). Washington, DC: US Department of Health and Human Services. Retrieved June 3, 2011, from http://pubs.niaaa.nih.gov/publications/Practitioner/CliniciansGuide2005/guide.pdf

Newcomb, M. D., Maddahian, E., & Bentler, P. M. (1986). Risk factors for drug use among adolescents: Concurrent and longitudinal analyses. *American Journal of Public Health, 76* (5), 525–531.

Newton, N., Andrews, G., Teesson, M., & Vogl, L. (2009b). Delivering prevention for alcohol and cannabis using the internet. A cluster randomized controlled trial. *Preventive Medicine, 48* (6), 579–584.

Newton, N., Vogl, L., Teesson, M., & Andrews, G. (2009a). CLIMATE Schools: Alcohol module: Cross-validation of a school-based prevention program for alcohol misuse. *Australian and New Zealand Journal of Psychiatry, 43* (3), 201–207.

Nicholas, R. (2005). *The role of alcohol in family violence.* Canberra: Australasian Centre for Policing Research.

Nordstrom, B. R., & Levin, F. R. (2007). Treatment of cannabis use disorders: A review of the literature. *American Journal on Addictions, 16* (5), 331–342.

Nutt, D. (1997). The neurochemistry of addiction. *Human Psychopharmacology, 12*, s53–s58.

Nutt, D., Robbins, T., Stimson, G., Ince, M., & Jackson, A. (2007). *Drugs and the future: Brain science, addiction and society.* London: Academic Press.

Office of National Drug Control Policy. (2010). *Drug facts: Street terms.* Rockville, MD: ONDCP. Retrieved June 3, 2011, from http://www.whitehousedrugpolicy.gov/streetterms/Default.asp

Olmsted, C. L., & Kockler, D. R. (2008).

Topiramate for alcohol dependence. *Annals of Pharmacotherapy, 42* (10), 1475–1480.

Pacher, P., Batkai, S., & Kunos, G. (2006). The endocannabinoid system as an emerging target of pharmacotherapy. *Pharmacological Reviews, 58* (3), 389–462.

Pantalon, M. V., Nich, C., Frankforter, T., Carroll, K. M., & University of Rhode Island Change (2002). The URICA as a measure of motivation to change among treatment-seeking individuals with concurrent alcohol and cocaine problems. *Psychology of Addictive Behaviors, 16* (4), 299–307.

Parsons, A. C., Shraim, M., Inglis, J., Aveyard, P., & Hajek, P. (2009). Interventions for preventing weight gain after smoking cessation. *Cochrane Database of Systematic Reviews, 1*, CD006219. Retrieved May 31, 2011, from http://www2.cochrane.org/reviews/en/ab006219.html

Pedersen, C. M. (1986). Hospital admissions from a non-medical alcohol detoxification unit. *Australian Drug and Alcohol Review, 5*, 133–137.

Petry, N. M., Alessi, S. M., & Hanson, T. (2007). Contingency management improves abstinence and quality of life in cocaine abusers. *Journal of Consulting & Clinical Psychology, 75* (2), 307–315.

Platt, J. J. (1997). *Cocaine addiction: Theory, research, and treatment.* Cambridge, MA: Harvard University Press.

Pomerleau, O., & Pomerleau, C. (1988). *Nicotine replacement – A critical evaluation.* New York: Alan R. Liss Publishers.

Postel, M. G., de Jong, C. A. J., & de Haan, H. A. (2005). Does e-therapy for problem drinking reach hidden populations? *American Journal of Psychiatry, 162* (12), 2393.

Prins, A., Ouimette, P., Kimerling, R., Cameron, R. P., Hugelshofer, D. S., Shaw-Hegwer, J., et al. (2003). The primary care PTSD screen (PC-PTSD):

Development and operating characteristics. *Primary Care Psychiatry,* 9 (1), 9–14.

Project MATCH Research Group. (1997). Matching alcoholism treatments to client heterogeneity: Project MATCH posttreatment drinking outcomes. *Journal of Studies on Alcohol, 58,* 7–29.

Proudfoot, H., Baillie, A. J., & Teesson, M. (2006). The structure of alcohol dependence in the community. *Drug and Alcohol Dependence, 81* (1), 21–26.

Proudfoot, H., & Teesson, M. (2000). *Investing in drug and alcohol treatment* (Technical Report No. 91). Sydney: National Drug and Alcohol Research Centre, University of New South Wales.

Proudfoot, H., & Teesson, M. (2001). *Who seeks treatment for alcohol dependence? Findings from the Australian National Survey of Mental Health and Wellbeing* (NDARC Technical Report No. 122). Sydney: National Drug and Alcohol Research Centre, University of New South Wales.

Proudfoot, H., Vogl, L., Swift, W., Martin, G., & Copeland, J. (2010). Development of a short cannabis problems questionnaire for adolescents in the community. *Addictive Behaviors, 35,* 734–737.

Queensland Health. (2004). *Psychostimulants: Information for health workers.* Queensland: Queensland Health. Retrieved June 3, 2011, from http://www.dassa.sa.gov.au/webdata/resources/files/psychostimulants.pdf

Raistrick, D., Dunbar, G., & Davidson, R. (1983). Development of a questionnaire to measure alcohol dependence. *British Journal of Addiction, 78,* 89–95.

Rawson, R. A., & Tennant, F. S. (1984). Five year follow-up of opiate addicts with naltrexone and behaviour therapy. *NIDA Research Monographs, 49,* 289–295.

Reda, A. A., Kaper, J., Fikretler, H., Severens, J. L., & van Schayck, C. P. (2009). Healthcare financing systems for increasing the use of tobacco dependence treatment. *Cochrane Database of Systematic Reviews, 2,* CD004305.

Regier, D. A., Farmer, M. E., Rae, D. S., Locke, B. Z., Keith, S. J., Judd, L. L., et al. (1990). Comorbidity of mental disorders with alcohol and other drug abuse: Results from the Epidemiologic Catchment Area (ECA) study. *Journal of the American Medical Association, 264,* 2511–2518.

Regier, D. A., Narrow, W. E., Rae, D. S., Manderscheid, R. W., Locke, B. Z., & Goodwin, F. K. (1993). The de facto US mental and addictive disorders service system: Epidemiologic Catchment Area prospective study 1-year prevalence rates of disorders and services. *Archives of General Psychiatry, 50,* 85–94.

Rehm, J., Gmel, G., Sempos, C. T., & Trevisan, M. (2003). Alcohol-related morbidity and mortality. *Alcohol Research & Health: The Journal of the National Institute on Alcohol Abuse & Alcoholism, 27* (1), 39–51.

Rehm, J., Mathers, C., Popova, S., Thavorncharoensap, M., Teerawattananon, Y., & Patra, J. (2009). Global burden of disease and injury and economic cost attributable to alcohol use and alcohol-use disorders. *Lancet, 373* (9682), 2223–2233.

Rehm, J., Taylor, B., & Room, R. (2006). Global burden of disease from alcohol, illicit drugs and tobacco. *Drug & Alcohol Review, 25* (6), 503–513.

Ridolfo, B., & Stevenson, C. (2001). *The quantification of drug-caused mortality and morbidity in Australia, 1998.* Canberra: Health and Welfare.

Rigotti, N., Munafo, M. R., & Stead Lindsay, F. (2007). Interventions for smoking cessation in hospitalised patients. *Cochrane Database of Systematic Reviews, 3,* CD001837. Retrieved May 31, 2011, from http://

www2.cochrane.org/reviews/en/ab001837.html

Riper, H., Kramer, J., Keuken, M., Smit, F., Schippers, G., & Cuijpers, P. (2008). Predicting successful treatment outcome of web-based self-help for problem drinkers: Secondary analysis from a randomized controlled trial. *Journal of Medical Internet Research, 10* (4), e46.

Robins, L. (1978). Sturdy childhood predictors of adult anti-social behavior: Replications from longitudinal studies. *Psychological Medicine, 8,* 611–622.

Robins, L. N., & Regier, D. A. (Eds.). (1991). *Psychiatric disorders in America: The Epidemiologic Catchment Area Study.* New York: The Free Press.

Roerecke, M., & Rehm, J. (2010). Irregular heavy drinking occasions and risk of ischemic heart disease: A systematic review and meta-analysis. *American Journal of Epidemiology, 171* (6), 633–644.

Rogers, G., Elston, J., Garside, R., Roome, C., Taylor, R., Younger, P., et al. (2009). *The harmful health effects of recreational ecstasy: A systematic review of observational evidence.* Winchester: Health Technology Assessment.

Rohsenow, D. J., Monti, P. M., Rubonis, A. V., Gulliver, S. B., Colby, S. M., Binkoff, J. A., et al. (2001). Cue exposure with coping skills training and communication skills training for alcohol dependence: 6- and 12-month outcomes. *Addiction, 96* (8), 1161–1174.

Romach, M., Glue, P., Kampman, K., Kaplan, H., Somer, G., Poole, S., et al. (1999). Attenuation of the euphoric effects of cocaine by the dopamine D1/D5 antagonist Ecopipam (SCH 39166). *Archives of General Psychiatry, 56,* 1101–1106.

Room, R. (2005). Stigma, social inequality and alcohol and drug use. *Drug & Alcohol Review, 24* (2), 143–155.

Roozen, H. G., Boulogne, J. J., van Tulder, M. W., van den Brink, W., De Jong, C.

A. J., & Kerkhof, A. J. F. M. (2004). A systematic review of the effectiveness of the community reinforcement approach in alcohol, cocaine and opioid addiction. *Drug & Alcohol Dependence, 74* (1), 1–13.

Rösner, S., Hackle-Herrwerth, A., Leutch, S., Vecchi, S., Srisurapanont, M., & Soyka, M. (2010). Opioid antagonists for alcohol dependence. *Cochrane Database of Systematic Reviews, 12,* CD001867. Retrieved June 3, 2011, from http://www2.cochrane.org/reviews/en/ab001867.html

Ross, J. (Ed.). (2007). *Illicit drug use in Australia: Epidemiology, use patterns and associated harm* (2nd ed.). Canberra: Australian Government Department of Health and Ageing.

Roth, A., Hogan, I., & Farren, C. (1997). Naltrexone plus group therapy for the treatment of opiate-abusing health-care professionals. *Journal of Substance Abuse Treatment, 14* (1), 19–22.

Royal College of Physicians. (2005). *Cannabis and cannabis-based medicines: Potential benefits and risks to health. Report of a working party.* London: Royal College of Physicians.

Rubak, S., Sandbaek, A., Lauritzen, T., & Christensen, B. (2005). Motivational interviewing: A systematic review and meta-analysis. *British Journal of General Practice, 55* (513), 305–312.

Russell, M., & Bigler, L. (1979). Screening for alcohol-related problems in an outpatient obstetric-gynecologic clinic. *American Journal of Obstetrics and Gynaecology, 134,* 4–12.

Saitz, R. (2007). Treatment of alcohol and other drug dependence. *Liver Transplantation, 13* (11 Suppl. 2), S59–64.

Saunders, J., Aasland, O., Babor, T., de le Fuente, J., & Grant, M. (1993). Development of the Alcohol Use Disorders Identification Test (AUDIT): WHO Collaborative Project on Early Detection of Persons with Harmful

Alcohol Consumption – II. *Addiction, 88*, 791–803.

Schinke, S. P., Tepavac, L., & Cole, K. C. (2000). Preventing substance use among Native American youth: Three-year results. *Addictive Behaviors, 25* (3), 387–397.

Schuckit, M. A. (1996). Recent developments in the pharmacotherapy of alcohol dependence. *Journal of Consulting and Clinical Psychology, 64* (4), 669–676.

Scott, K. M., McGee, M. A., Browne, M. A. O., & Wells, J. E. (2006). Mental disorder comorbidity in Te Rau Hinengaro: The New Zealand Mental Health Survey. *Australian and New Zealand Journal of Psychiatry, 40* (10), 875–881.

Shanahan, M., Havard, A., Teesson, M., Mills, K., Williamson, A., & Ross, J. (2006). Patterns and costs of treatment for heroin dependence over 12 months: Findings from the Australian Treatment Outcome Study. *Australian & New Zealand Journal of Public Health, 30* (4), 305–311.

Shearer, J., Darke, S., Rodgers, C., Slade, T., van Beek, I., Lewis, J., et al. (2009). A double-blind, placebo-controlled trial of modafinil (200 mg/day) for methamphetamine dependence. *Addiction, 104* (2), 224–233.

Shoptaw, S. J., Kao, U., Heinzerling, K., & Ling, W. (2009). Treatment for amphetamine withdrawal. *Cochrane Database of Systematic Reviews, 2,* CD003021.

Simpson, D., & Sells, S. (1982). Effectiveness of treatment for drug abuse: An overview of the DARP research program. *Advances in Alcohol and Substance Abuse, 2,* 7–29.

Singleton, N., Bumpstead, R., O'Brien, M., Lee, A., & Meltzer, H. (2001). *Psychiatric morbidity among adults living in private households, 2000.* London: Social Survey Division of the Office for National Statistics.

Singleton, N., Bumpstead, R., O'Brien, M., Lee, A., & Meltzer, H. (2003). Psychiatric morbidity among adults living in private households, 2000. *International Review of Psychiatry, 15* (1–2), 65–73.

Sitharthan, T., & Kavanagh, D. J. (1991). Role of self efficacy in predicting outcomes for a programme for controlled drinking. *Drug and Alcohol Dependence, 27* (1), 87–94.

Skinner, H. A., & Horn, J. L. (1984). *Alcohol Dependence Scale (ADS): Users guide.* Toronto: ARF.

Skinner, M. D., & Aubin, H.-J. (2010). Craving's place in addiction theory: Contributions of the major models. *Neuroscience & Biobehavioral Reviews, 34* (4), 606–623.

Slade, T., Johnston, A., Oakley Browne, M. A., Andrews, G., & Whiteford, H. (2009). 2007 National Survey of Mental Health and Wellbeing: Methods and key findings. *Australian and New Zealand Journal of Psychiatry, 43* (7), 594–605.

Smelson, D. A., McGee Caulfield, E., Bergstein, P., & Engelhart, C. (1999). Initial validation of the Voris Cocaine Craving Scale: A preliminary report. *Journal of Clinical Psychology, 55* (1), 135–139.

Smith, D. E., & Gay, G. R. (1972). *"It's so good, don't even try it once": Heroin in perspective.* Englewood Cliffs, NJ: Prentice-Hall.

Smith, L. A., Gates, S., & Foxcroft, D. (2006). Therapeutic communities for substance related disorder. *Cochrane Database of Systematic Reviews, 1,* CD005338. Retrieved June 1, 2011, from http://www2.cochrane.org/reviews/en/ab005338.html

Sobell, M. B., & Sobell, L. C. (1995). Controlled drinking after 25 years: How important was the great debate?

Addiction, 90 (9), 1149–1153; discussion 1157–1177.

Spooner, C., & Hetherington, K. (2006). *Social determinants of drug use.* Sydney: National Drug & Alcohol Research Centre.

Srisurapanont, M., Jarusuraisin, N., & Kittirattanapaiboon, P. (2008). Treatment for amphetamine dependence and abuse. *Cochrane Database of Systematic Reviews, 3,* CD003022.

Stade, B. C., Bailey, C., Dzendoletas, D., Sgro, M., Dowswell, T., & Bennett, D. (2009). Psychological and/or educational interventions for reducing alcohol consumption in pregnant women and women planning pregnancy. *Cochrane Database of Systematic Reviews, 2,* CD004228.

Stafford, J., Degenhardt, L., Black, E., Bruno, R., Buckingham, K., Fetherston, J., et al. (2006). *Australian drug trends 2005. Findings from the illicit drug reporting system (IDRS)* (NDARC Monograph No. 59). Sydney: National Drug and Alcohol Research Centre.

Stahl, S. (1996). *Essential psychopharmacology.* Cambridge: Cambridge University Press.

Stead, L. F., Bergson, G., & Lancaster, T. (2008a). Physician advice for smoking cessation. *Cochrane Database of Systematic Reviews, 2,* CD000165. Retrieved May 31, 2011, from http://www2.cochrane.org/reviews/en/ab000165.html

Stead, L. F., & Lancaster, T. (2005). Group behaviour therapy programmes for smoking cessation. *Cochrane Database of Systematic Reviews, 2,* CD001007. Retrieved May 31, 2011, from http://www2.cochrane.org/reviews/en/ab001007.html

Stead, L. F., & Lancaster, T. (2006). Nicobrevin for smoking cessation. *Cochrane Database of Systematic Reviews, 2,* CD005990. Retrieved May 31, 2011, from http://www2.cochrane.org/reviews/en/ab005990.html

Stead, L. F., & Lancaster, T. (2007). Interventions to reduce harm from continued tobacco use. *Cochrane Database of Systematic Reviews, 3,* CD005231. Retrieved May 31, 2011, from http://www2.cochrane.org/reviews/en/ab005231.html

Stead, L. F., Perera, R., Bullen, C., Mant, D., & Lancaster, T. (2008b). Nicotine replacement therapy for smoking cessation. *Cochrane Database of Systematic Reviews, 1,* CD000146. Retrieved May 31, 2011, from http://www2.cochrane.org/reviews/en/ab000146.html

Stead, L. F., Perera, R., & Lancaster, T. (2006). Telephone counselling for smoking cessation. *Cochrane Database of Systematic Reviews, 3,* CD002850. Retrieved May 31, 2011, from http://www2.cochrane.org/reviews/en/ab002850.html

Stine, S., & Kosten, T. (Eds.) (1997). *Treatments for opioid dependence.* New York: Guilford Press.

Stockwell, T., Bolt, L., Milner, I., Russell, G., Bolderston, H., & Pugh, P. (1991). Home detoxification from alcohol: Its safety and efficacy in comparison with inpatient care. *Alcohol & Alcoholism, 26* (5/6), 645–650.

Stockwell, T., Murphy, D., & Hodgson, R. (1983). The severity of alcohol dependence questionnaire: Its use, reliability and validity. *British Journal of Addiction, 78,* 145–155.

Stockwell, T., Sitharthan, T., McGrath, D., & Lang, E. (1994). The measurement of alcohol dependence and impaired control in community samples. *Addiction, 89,* 167–174.

Sutherland, G., Edwards, G., Taylor, C., Phillips, G., Gossop, M., & Brady, R. (1986). The measurement of opiate dependence. *British Journal of Addiction, 81,* 485–494.

Swift, W., Copeland, J., & Hall, W. (1997). *Cannabis dependence among long-term users in Sydney, Australia* (Technical Report No. 47). Sydney: National Drug and Alcohol Research Centre.

Swift, W., Copeland, J., & Hall, W. (1998). Choosing a diagnostic cut-off for cannabis dependence. *Addiction, 93* (11), 1681–1692.

Szegedi, A., Lorch, B., Scheurich, A., Ruppe, A., Hautzinger, M., & Wetzel, H. (2000). Cue exposure in alcohol dependent patients: Preliminary evidence for different types of cue reactivity. *Journal of Neural Transmission, 107* (6), 721–730.

Tapert, S. F., Caldwell, L., & Burke, C. (2005). Alcohol and the adolescent brain. Human studies. *Alcohol Research and Health, 28,* 205–212.

Teesson, M., Hall, W., Slade, T., Mills, K., Grove, R., Mewton, L., et al. (2010). Prevalence and correlates of DSM-IV alcohol abuse and dependence in Australia: Findings of the 2007 National Survey of Mental Health and Wellbeing. *Addiction, 105* (12), 2085–2094.

Teesson, M., Havard, A., Fairbairn, S., Ross, J., Lynskey, M., & Darke, S. (2005). Depression among entrants to treatment for heroin dependence in the Australian Treatment Outcome Study (ATOS): Prevalence, correlates and treatment seeking. *Drug & Alcohol Dependence, 78* (3), 309–315.

Teesson, M., Havard, A., Ross, J., & Darke, S. (2006). Outcomes after detoxification for heroin dependence: Findings from the Australian Treatment Outcome Study (ATOS). *Drug & Alcohol Review, 25* (3), 241–247.

Teesson, M., Hodder, T., & Buhrich, N. (2003). Alcohol and other drug use disorders among homeless people in Australia. *Substance Use and Misuse, 38* (3–6), 463–474.

Teesson, M., Lynskey, M., Manor, B., & Baillie, A. (2002). The structure of cannabis dependence in the community. *Drug and Alcohol Dependence, 68,* 255–262.

Teesson, M., Mills, K., Ross, J., Darke, S., Williamson, A., & Havard, A. (2008). The impact of treatment on 3 year outcomes for heroin dependence: Findings from the Australian Treatment Outcome Study (ATOS). *Addiction, 103,* 80–88.

Theobald, H., Johansson, S. E., Bygren, L. O., & Engfeldt, P. (2001). The effects of alcohol consumption on mortality and morbidity: A 26-year follow-up study. *Journal of Studies on Alcohol, 62* (6), 783–789.

Thun, M. J., Peto, R., Lopez, A. D., Monaco, J. H., Henley, S. J., Heath, C. W. Jr., & Doll, R. (0000). Alcohol consumption and mortality among middle-aged and elderly US adults. *New England Journal of Medicine, 337* (24), 1705–1714.

Topp, L., & Mattick, R. P. (1997). Choosing a cut-off on the Severity of Dependence Scale (SDS) for amphetamine users. *Addiction, 92* (7), 839–845.

True, W., Xian, H., Scherrer, J., Madden, P., Bucholz, K., Heath, A., et al. (1999). Common genetic vulnerability for nicotine and alcohol dependence. *Archives of General Psychiatry, 56,* 655–661.

Tsuang, M. T., Lyons, M. J., Meyer, J. M., Doyle, T., Eisen, S. A., Goldberg, J., et al. (1998). Co-occurrence of abuse of different drugs in men: The role of drug-specific and shared vulnerabilities. *Archives of General Psychiatry, 55* (11), 967–972.

UKATT Research Team. (2005). Cost effectiveness of treatment for alcohol problems: Findings of the randomised UK alcohol treatment trial (UKATT). *BMJ, 331* (7516), 544.

UKATT Research Team. (2008). UK Alcohol Treatment Trial: Client-treatment matching effects. *Addiction*, *103* (2), 228–238.

United Nations Office on Drugs and Crime (UNODC). (2009). *World drug report*. New York: United Nations.

US Department of Health and Human Services. (2004). *The health consequences of smoking*. Washington, DC: US Department of Health and Human Services, Centers for Disease Control and Prevention.

US Department of Health and Human Services. (2006). *The health consequences of involuntary exposure to tobacco smoke*. Washington, DC: US Department of Health and Human Services, Centers for Disease Control and Prevention.

Ussher, M. H., Taylor, A., & Faulkner, G. (2008). Exercise interventions for smoking cessation. *Cochrane Database of Systematic Reviews*, *4*, CD002295. Retrieved June 4, 2011, from http://www2.cochrane.org/reviews/en/ab002295.html

Vasilaki, E. I., Hosier, S. G., & Cox, W. M. (2006). The efficacy of motivational interviewing as a brief intervention for excessive drinking: A meta-analytic review. *Alcohol & Alcoholism*, *41* (3), 328–335.

Vedel, E., Emmelkamp, P. M. G., & Schippers, G. M. (2008). Individual cognitive-behavioral therapy and behavioral couples therapy in alcohol use disorder: A comparative evaluation in community-based addiction treatment centers. *Psychotherapy & Psychosomatics*, *77* (5), 280–288.

Veilleux, J. C., Colvin, P. J., Anderson, J., York, C., & Heinz, A. J. (2010). A review of opioid dependence treatment: Pharmacological and psychosocial. *Clinical Psychology Review*, *30*, 155–166.

Vernon, M. L. (2010). A review of computer-based alcohol problem services designed for the general public. *Journal of Substance Abuse Treatment 38*, 203–211.

Vogl, L., Teesson, M., Andrews, G., Dillon, P., & Steadman, B. (2009). A computerized harm minimization prevention program for alcohol misuse and related harms: Randomized controlled trial. *Addiction*, *104*, 564–575.

Vogt, F., Hall, S., & Marteau, T. M. (2007). General practitioners' beliefs about effectiveness and intentions to recommend smoking cessation services: Qualitative and quantitative studies. *BMC Family Practice*, *8*, 39.

Wagena, E. J., van der Meer, R. M., Ostelo, R. J. W. G., Jacobs, J. E., & van Schayck, C. P. (2004). The efficacy of smoking cessation strategies in people with chronic obstructive pulmonary disease: Results from a systematic review. *Respiratory Medicine*, *98* (9), 805–815.

Walsh, S. L., Stoops, W. W., Moody, D. E., Lin, S.-N., & Bigelow, G. E. (2009). Repeated dosing with oral cocaine in humans: Assessment of direct effects, withdrawal, and pharmacokinetics. *Experimental & Clinical Psychopharmacology*, *17* (4), 205–216.

Ward, J., Mattick, R. P., & Hall, W. (Eds.). (1998). *Methadone maintenance treatment and other opioid replacement therapies*. Amsterdam: OPA.

Washton, A. M., Gold, M. S., & Pottash, A. C. (1984). Naltrexone in addicted physicians and business executives. *NIDA Research Monograph*, *55*, 185–190.

Webb, G., Shakeshaft, A., Sanson-Fisher, R., & Havard, A. (2009). A systematic review of work-place interventions for alcohol-related problems. *Addiction*, *104* (3), 365–377.

Weiss, R. D., & Kueppenbender, K. D. (2006). Combining psychosocial treatment with pharmacotherapy for alcohol dependence. *Journal of Clinical Psychopharmacology*, *26* (Suppl. 1), S37–42.

Wells, J. E., Oakley Browne, M. A., Scott, K. M., McGee, M. A., Baxter, J., & Kokaua, J. (2006). Prevalence, interference with life and severity of 12 month DSM-IV disorders in Te Rau Hinengaro: The New Zealand Mental Health Survey. *Australian and New Zealand Journal of Psychiatry*, 40 (10), 845–854.

Welsh, I. (1993). *Trainspotting*, London: Random House.

West, R. (1989). The psychological basis of addiction. *International Review of Psychiatry*, 1, 71–80.

West, R. (2004). Assessment of dependence and motivation to stop smoking. *BMJ*, 328 (7435), 338–339.

West, R. (2006). *Theory of addiction*. Oxford: Blackwell Publishing.

West, R., & Ussher, M. (2010). Is the ten-item Questionnaire of Smoking Urges (QSU-brief) more sensitive to abstinence than shorter craving measures? *Psychopharmacology*, 28 (3), 427–432.

White, A. R., Rampes, H., Liu, J. P., Stead, L. F., & Campbell, J. (2011). Acupuncture and related interventions for smoking cessation. *Cochrane Database of Systematic Reviews*, 1, CD000009. Retrieved June 4, 2011, from http://www2.cochrane.org/reviews/en/ab000009.html

Williams, B. T., & Drummond, D. C. (1994). The Alcohol Problems Questionnaire: Reliability and validity. *Drug & Alcohol Dependence*, 35 (3), 239–243.

World Health Organization. (1993). *The ICD-10 classification of mental and behavioural disorders – Diagnostic criteria for research*. Geneva: World Health Organization.

World Health Organization. (2002). *World Health Report 2002: Reducing risks, promoting healthy life*. Geneva: WHO. Retrieved June 4, 2011, from http://www.who.int/whr/2002/en/whr02_en.pdf

World Health Organization. (2004a). *Global status report on alcohol*. Geneva: WHO.

World Health Organization. (2004b). *Neuroscience of psychoactive substance use and dependence*. Geneva: Switzerland.

World Health Organization Brief Intervention Study Group. (1996). A cross-national trial of brief interventions with heavy drinkers. *American Journal of Public Health*, 86 (7), 948–955.

Yudko, E., Lozhkina, O., & Fouts, A. (2007). A comprehensive review of the psychometric properties of the Drug Abuse Screening Test. *Journal of Substance Abuse Treatment*, 32 (2), 189–198.

Zvolensky, M. J., Bernstein, A., Marshall, E. C., & Feldner, M. T. (2006). Panic attacks, panic disorder, and agoraphobia: Associations with substance use, abuse, and dependence. *Current Psychiatry Reports*, 8 (4), 279–285.

Author index

Subject index

Disulfiram (Antabuse), 67–68
Divalproex, 68, 92
Dopamine reward system, 36, 38, 39
Dopaminergic agents, 68
Drug abuse, 8–9, 15
Drug Abuse Screening Test (DAST), 89
Drug dependence
  comorbidity, 14, 15, 16–18, 19–20
  definitions, 6–7, 15
  diagnosis, 7–8, 9–11
  studies and surveys, 15, 16–20
Drug Impairment Rating Scale, 112
Drugs
  attitudes to, 12
  causes of problems, 6–7
  classes of drugs, 3
  definitions, 2, 12
  effects of, 4–5
  illegality, 118
  mortality and morbidity, 22–31
  psychotropic drugs, 2–3
  reasons for use, 5
  "street" names, 2–3
DSM-IV, *see Diagnostic and Statistical Manual of Mental Disorders*

Ecstasy, 111–112
  abuse, 10
  adverse health and psychological effects, 29
  assessment, 112–113
  comorbidity, 113
  effects, 5
  molecular and cellular sites of action, 37
  "street" names, 3
  treatment, 115
Endogenous opioid system, 38, 39
Epidemiologic Catchment Area (ECA) study (USA), 13–15
Ethnicity, 18
European Study of the Epidemiology of Mental Disorders (ESEMeD), 17
Exercise, 82

Fagerström Test for Nicotine Dependence, 74, 75, 79
Family and marital therapy (FMT), 63–64
Feedback on bio-markers, 82

Fetal alcohol syndrome (FAS), 25
Financial compensation, 82
Fluoxetine, 92, 114

Gender
  and addiction, 14, 15, 16, 17, 18
  mortality and morbidity, 23, 49, 73
  and treatment, 58
Genetic factors, 40–41
  identifying specific risk genes, 41
  specificity of drug effects, 41
GHB (gamma-hydroxybutyric acid), 59, 68–69
Global Burden of Disease (GBD) studies, 21–22, 26, 73, 117

Hallucinogens, 3
Hashish, 87, *see also* Cannabis
Health consequences, 21–33
  alcohol-related mortality and morbidity, 22–26, 49
  controversies on positive effects, 31–33
  illicit drug-related mortality and morbidity, 27–31
  tobacco-related mortality and morbidity, 22, 26–27, 73
Heroin, 99, 100
  adverse health and psychological effects, 30
  assessment, 100
  detoxification, 102, 103
  effects, 4–5
  pharmacotherapies, 106–109
  psychosocial treatment, 105
  "street" names, 3
  withdrawal symptoms, 102
Heroin prescription, 108
Hypnotherapy, 82

Illicit drugs
  moral issues, 118
  mortality and morbidity, 29–31
Inhalants, 3
Instrumental behaviour, 42

Kessler's 10 Psychological Distress Scale (K10), 54, 113